CRAFTING QUALITATIVE RESEARCH QUESTIONS

CRAFTING QUALITATIVE RESEARCH QUESTIONS

A PREQUEL TO DESIGN

Elizabeth (Betsy) A. Baker

University of Missouri

Los Angeles | London | New Delhi
Singapore | Washington DC | Melbourne

QUALITATIVE RESEARCH METHODS SERIES

Series Editor: David L. Morgan, *Portland State University*

The ***Qualitative Research Methods Series*** currently consists of 62 volumes that address essential aspects of using qualitative methods across social and behavioral sciences. These widely used books provide valuable resources for a broad range of scholars, researchers, teachers, students, and community-based researchers.

The series publishes volumes that:

- Address topics of current interest to the field of qualitative research.
- Provide practical guidance and assistance with collecting and analyzing qualitative data.
- Highlight essential issues in qualitative research, including strategies to address those issues.
- Add new voices to the field of qualitative research.

A key characteristic of the Qualitative Research Methods Series is an emphasis on both a "*why*" and a "*how-to*" perspective, so that readers will understand the purposes and motivations behind a method, as well as the practical and technical aspects of using that method. These relatively short and inexpensive books rely on a cross-disciplinary approach, and they typically include examples from practice; tables, boxes, and figures; discussion questions; application activities; and further reading sources.

New and forthcoming volumes in the Series include:

Introduction to Cognitive Ethnography and Systematic Field Work
G. Mark Schoepfle

Narrative as Topic and Method in Social Research
Donileen R. Loseke

Crafting Qualitative Research Questions: A Prequel to Design
Elizabeth (Betsy) A. Baker

Photovoice for Social Justice: Visual Representation in Action
Jean M. Breny and Shannon L. McMorrow

Qualitative Instrument Design: A Guide for the Novice Researcher
Felice D. Billups

How to Write a Phenomenological Dissertation
Katarzyna Peoples

Reflexive Narrative: Self-Inquiry Towards Self-Realization and Its Performance
Christopher Johns

Hybrid Ethnography: Online, Offline, and In Between
Liz Przybylski

For information on how to submit a proposal for the Series, please contact:

- David L. Morgan, Series Editor: morgand@pdx.edu
- Leah Fargotstein, Senior Acquisitions Editor, SAGE: leah.fargotstein@sagepub.com

FOR INFORMATION:

SAGE Publications, Inc.
2455 Teller Road
Thousand Oaks, California 91320
E-mail: order@sagepub.com

SAGE Publications Ltd.
1 Oliver's Yard
55 City Road
London, EC1Y 1SP
United Kingdom

SAGE Publications India Pvt. Ltd.
B 1/I 1 Mohan Cooperative Industrial Area
Mathura Road, New Delhi 110 044
India

SAGE Publications Asia-Pacific Pte. Ltd.
18 Cross Street #10-10/11/12
China Square Central
Singapore 048423

Acquisitions Editor: Helen Salmon
Product Associate: Kenzie Offley
Production Editor: Vijayakumar
Copy Editor: Christobel Colleen Hopman
Typesetter: TNQ Technologies
Proofreader: Benny Willy Stephen
Indexer: TNQ Technologies
Cover Designer: Janet Kiesel
Marketing Manager: Victoria Velasquez

Printed in the United States of America

This book is printed on acid-free paper.

ISBN 978-1-0718-1913-5

21 22 23 24 25 10 9 8 7 6 5 4 3 2 1

I dedicate this book to my parents, Maude Bragg Dickson Baker (1927–2020) and Walter Baker, Jr. (1928–2021), who constantly observed and wondered: Why does one candle burn faster than the other, how can a coupe be designed for increased headroom in the backseat, what will foster self-efficacy among preschool children? Wonderment was the staple of childhood and adulthood conversations with my parents. Is it any wonder they inspired me to become a researcher?

BRIEF CONTENTS

DETAILED CONTENTS

LIST OF TABLES

LIST OF WORKSHEETS

ACKNOWLEDGMENTS

SAGE and the author are grateful for feedback from the following reviewers in the development of this text:

Ljubinka Andonoska, University of Texas at El Paso

Wayne A. Babchuk, University of Nebraska–Lincoln

Christina Convertino, University of Texas at El Paso

Leanne M. Dzubinski, Biola University

Kathryn Herr, Montclair State University

Elizabeth M. Lee, Ohio University

Raquel C. Sanchez, University of California

Julie Slayton, University of Southern California

Margaret-Mary Sulenic Dowell, Louisiana State University

APPRECIATION

I want to thank Helen Salmon for her vision and ushering this book through the process from prospectus to publication. Thank you for garnering invaluable feedback. Every iteration advanced the fulfillment of my vision.

I want to thank David Morgan. I admired your work before this project. The opportunity to work with you was my honor. Your guidance was targeted and insightful. The resultant book is better because of you.

I want to thank Charles (Chuck) Kinzer, my doctoral advisor and friend. Chuck challenged me to think like a researcher. I'm sure it would've been much easier to leave me in my mediocrity.

I want to thank Deborah (Debbie) Rowe who methodologically captivated me during my first graduate course in qualitative research, helped me ponder philosophical implications of my research design decisions, and consistently conducts research that continues to intrigue me.

I want to thank the graduate students with whom I have worked to craft qualitative research questions and design qualitative studies. Your work and insights continue to inspire me.

ABOUT THE AUTHOR

Elizabeth (Betsy) A. Baker is a Professor of Literacy Studies at the University of Missouri, Past President of the Literacy Research Association, former coeditor of *Literacy Research: Theory, Method and Practice (LRTMP)*, and the creator, executive producer, and cohost of the *Voice of Literacy* podcast (http://www.voiceofliteracy.org/). She began her career as a second-grade teacher in Greenville, SC, where she became fascinated by literacy acquisition and development. She holds a BA in Elementary Education from Furman University, and an MEd and EdD in Reading/Literacy Education from Vanderbilt University.

Her research agenda takes place at the substantive crossroads of literacy, technology, and teacher education while drawing from sociocultural, cognitive, and systems theories. She seeks to harness the affordances of varied technologies while mitigating challenges to teaching and learning. Research projects include the federally funded development of ChALK (Children as Literacy Kases), naturalistic explorations of the nature of literacy in digital environments, analyses of the literacy learning and pedagogy supported by classroom websites, as well as *Talk to Read*©, a speech recognition project.

Among others, her research appears in *Reading Research Quarterly*, *Journal of Literacy Research*, *Language Arts*, *Journal of Early Childhood Literacy*, *NRC Yearbook* (now *LRTMP*), *Journal of Reading Education*, *Reading and Writing Quarterly*, *Journal of Technology and Teacher Education*, *Journal of Educational Multimedia and Hypermedia*, *Handbook of Research on the Societal Impact of Digital Media*, *Teacher Education Quarterly*, and her edited book, *The New Literacies: Multiple Perspectives on Research and Practice* with Guilford Press.

Her research, teaching, and service have been recognized by college, campus, state, national, and international awards including the Computers in Reading Research Award (International Literacy Association), Ernest L.

Boyer International Award for Excellence in Teaching, Learning, and Technology (International Conference on College Teaching and Learning), William T. Kemper Fellowship for Teaching Excellence (Kemper Foundation), and the Thomas Jefferson Award (President of the University of Missouri System).

INTRODUCTION

The essence of research design resides in your ability to articulate research questions. The research question is the progenitor of the study. A well-crafted question embodies all the design elements for your study, thereby providing the skeletal structure of your research design. Ask a well-crafted question and the design will fall into place. There is a myriad of valuable books that describe in wonderful detail the ins and outs of collecting and analyzing qualitative data. The purpose of this book is to give you the backstory; to describe what happens before you collect and analyze data; to describe what happens before you propose a study. This book focuses on how to formulate a well-crafted qualitative research question so that you are poised to pursue your passions, collaborate with others, propose designs in response to funding agencies, and serve as a reviewer who can provide succinct and poignant feedback to researchers. This book describes what happens before data are collected and analyzed. This book is the antecedent for conducting qualitative research. The purpose of this book is to provide the prequel to conducting a qualitative study.

For over 20 years, I have had the privilege of working with doctoral students as they crafted their own forays into qualitative research. In addition, I have wrestled with how to translate intriguing ideas into full-fledged research agendas for myself and teams of colleagues. As a result, I forged a research design **heuristic** (technique, strategy) that is based on formulating a qualitative research question. I refer to this heuristic as the Anatomy of a Qualitative Research Question. I think of it as a tool for strategic thinking; in this case, strategic thinking about qualitative research design. I offer this heuristic as a window into the microcosmic thinking of researchers as they formulate a line of qualitative research. I attempt to demystify the design process while providing a common heuristic that can be understood among researchers as they negotiate and evaluate design. I imagine that most researchers have heuristics that help them formulate research questions and craft research designs. I put this heuristic into writing to contribute to the corpus of qualitative research design resources.

1 THE ANATOMY OF QUALITATIVE RESEARCH QUESTIONS

CHAPTER OUTLINE

> *I am a first-semester doctoral student in Business. I have bachelor's and master's degrees in Business. I am interested in brand loyalty.*
>
> *I am a second-year doctoral student in Sports Psychology. I was a clinical psychologist for several years but want to focus on sports psychology. I am interested in the courage of CEOs.*
>
> *I am a master's student in Learning Technologies. I want to design educational software, so I am interested in users' experiences with interface screen clutter.*

These are typical introductions my students offer on the first night of a graduate seminar entitled, Introduction to Qualitative Research Methods. As graduate students, they bring a rich array of professional experiences as well as advanced coursework in their varied fields (e.g., Business, Sports Psychology, Learning

Technologies). As the instructor of a research methods course, it is my honor to help each student transform their professional interests into actionable research. As I listen, I wonder, how can I help these students formulate significant research questions, identify **research methods** (steps to follow as they collect and analyze data) that answer their questions, and prepare them to collect and analyze data that are **trustworthy** (incorporates strategies that help readers believe the findings of their study as well as discuss the limitations of their design; see Chapter 5: *Critique Trustworthiness*) and publishable? Similarly, whether I am having conversations with colleagues or planning for my next research project, I seek to refine the topic. In my experience, when someone expresses an interest, they have a hunch. They have an intuition that there is something significant to explore. I seek to hone a research question that preserves the kernel of intuition and maintains the zeal that gave birth to the topic of interest.

Challenged by transforming passions into research, over the years, I crafted a heuristic that I return to again and again. I work with students and colleagues to convert brand loyalty, CEO courage, interface clutter, and a full array of other passions from topics of interest to full-fledged studies. The heuristic is based on what I consider to be six fundamental components of qualitative research design. In other words, the heuristic represents a skeletal structure, or Anatomy, of research design. There may be other components and heuristics, nonetheless, I have found these six to be useful.

The purpose of this book is to introduce you to the Anatomy and support you as you translate your passions into a viable research question that incorporates the components of research design. The Anatomy may chafe your current concepts of research questions. I am hopeful, however, that when you use the Anatomy, you will be able to craft research questions that help you conduct corresponding studies efficiently and effectually. This book is a prequel to collecting and analyzing qualitative data. The focus is on formulating a qualitative research question—but not just any qualitative research question. Using the Anatomy, your question will embody the structural components of a well-crafted study. You will be poised to propose and conduct your study that I hope will illuminate your world.

To help you become familiar with the Anatomy, throughout this book, I reference and deconstruct a sample research question. The sample is derived from my dissertation that launched a significant portion of my research agenda through the ensuing decades. In this chapter, I dissect the sample question to reveal and briefly define the six parts of the Anatomy of a Qualitative Research Question. In the ensuing chapters, I revisit the parts of the Anatomy to consider their role in formulating a study and describe strategies you might use to refine and finalize your research question.

The parts can occur in varied sequences, should be used flexibly, and may even be omitted from the final research question. Nonetheless, I submit that researcher(s) should be cognizant of all six parts because they provide footholds for research design. This chapter might be likened to the box top of a jigsaw puzzle: it gives you the big picture. The purpose of Chapter 1 is to become familiar with the Anatomy by deconstructing a sample question and then practicing your familiarity by identifying the components of the Anatomy in seminal studies. In Chapter 2, I consider the role of **paradigms** (worldviews) in research design and challenge you to examine your paradigmatic assumptions. In Chapter 3, we dump the puzzle pieces on the table and start to work the puzzle. Specifically, I describe metacognitive strategies to help you transform your intuition into a robust research question. In Chapter 4, so you can see the Anatomy at work, I describe composite conversations I have with students and colleagues as we discuss topics of interest and formulate research questions. You get to be a fly on the wall and listen in as students/colleagues and I use the Anatomy. Finally, Chapter 5 is dedicated to converting your research question into a research proposal. I ponder the characteristics of innovative vs significant questions, provide a sample proposal template, leverage the Anatomy to formulate your rationale as well as evaluate related literature, revisit whether the parts of the Anatomy are in alignment, describe how to plan for trustworthiness, and finally highlight a few logistical points you might consider as you plan to conduct your study.

DECONSTRUCTING A SAMPLE QUESTION

Let's begin with the sample research question:

Given a postpositivist paradigm[1]*, what*[2] *is the nature of literacy*[3] *in a technology-rich fourth-grade classroom*[4] *from a sociocultural perspective*[5] *using ethnographic*[6] *research methods?*

The Anatomy of this research question consists of the following six parts:

1. Research paradigm: Postpositivist
2. Interrogative: What
3. Substance or Topic: Nature of literacy
4. Setting: Technology-rich fourth-grade classroom
5. Perspective: Sociocultural
6. Research tradition: Ethnographic Methods

I encourage novice researchers, and those who want to hone their design prowess, to practice by filling out these parts for several seminal studies (see Chapter 1: *Parse the Anatomy*, Suggested Activity #2, Worksheet 1.1). Consider how these parts are explicitly stated in the purpose of the study, articulated as research questions, and discussed in the manuscript. Again, some parts will appear in the research question while other parts may only appear in the manuscript. When you craft your own research question, I recommend that you fill out all six parts of the Anatomy, so you are aware of your own assumptions and the implications that each part has for your stated research question. Let me go through the sample.

Paradigm: Postpositivism

In Chapter 2, I attempt to explicate the role of paradigms in research design. I refer to research **paradigms** as the coalescence of **ontology** (philosophy of being), **epistemology** (philosophy of the existence of knowledge), **research tradition** (cohesive set of data collection and data analysis methods that purposely address specific types of questions while mitigating threats to trustworthiness), and **report genre** (distinctive literary style) (Hatch, 2002; Lincoln & Guba, 2005; see Appendix B). Paradigms encompass your worldview, your understanding of truth and reality. In the sample question, I am transparent with myself and my audience about my view of reality. I state upfront that my ontological and epistemological assumptions are rooted in postpositivism. The remainder of the Anatomy will therefore align with postpositivism. As detailed in Chapter 2, some basic tenets held by **postpositivists** include: reality is complex, systematic analysis can help us grapple with estimations of reality, the researcher and researched cannot be isolated therefore researcher bias must be acknowledged, findings are contextual and therefore the research report will include a rich description of the context to facilitate transferability (see Table 2.1). As a postpositivist, the interrogative, topic, setting, perspective(s), and research tradition will align with these tenets.

Often, research reports, especially journal articles, omit discussions of paradigmatic assumptions. Nonetheless, they exist. This part of the Anatomy, while often unstated, is fundamental to your research question. We ask the questions that we ask, we care about the questions we ask, because of our view of reality. While your research question may not explicitly state your paradigm, I encourage you to identify your assumptions about reality. I like to begin the methodology section of my proposals and reports with a paradigmatic statement that becomes fodder for the rationale of how I plan to collect and analyze data. Specifically, because the sample question was rooted in postpositivism, I systematically collected and analyzed my role in the setting, became a participant observer who maintained **prolonged engagement** (became part of the culture by being consistently present and involved in substantive activities with the participants; distinct from longitudinal methods in which researchers drop by over extended periods of time) so I could provide a **thick description** (sufficient description of the setting and social norms such that readers can compare to their own settings). Identify your paradigm. It will position you to articulate your question, refine your research design, and ultimately contend for the significance of your work. For additional discussion of paradigms, see Chapter 2.

Interrogative: What

In the sample question, the interrogative is *What*. One way to formulate research questions is to play with the interrogative. Is your study best conducted as a *What* question or a *Who, Where, When, Why, How* question? Interrogatives may appear innocuous. In reality, they shift the entire study including the focus/topic, perspective, related literature, rationale, and methods and may even imply paradigmatic assumptions. In Chapter 3, I will explore these implications in more depth.

Substance: Nature of Literacy

The third part of the Anatomy is the **topic** (substance). Carving out the substance helps you know what related literature to discuss. In this example, I discussed the literature regarding the nature of literacy—not literacy acquisition, not the effectiveness of using technology to support literacy development, nor an entire array of research about the integration of literacy and technology. As a reviewer for journals, I am often reminded that authors wrestle to identify their topic. Maybe a better way of saying this is that authors wrestle with how to narrow down their topic and carve out reports derived from broader studies. Qualitative researchers, in particular, are commonly interested in the complexities of reality. Numerous topics are viable within an area of study. However, for the purpose of design, researchers must carve out, hone in on the substance, topic, at hand. In my experience, this is not as easy as it sounds. Personally, I revise this part of the Anatomy several times while I formulate my overarching research question. For more details, see Chapter 4.

Setting: Technology-Rich Fourth-Grade Classroom

The fourth component of the Anatomy is self-explanatory. Where will this study occur? When you propose a study, the setting may be generic because you have not yet received Institutional Review Board (IRB) approval and therefore have not broached conversations with gatekeepers or potential participants. Nonetheless, you know the sort of location and participants with which you hope to work. When the sample study was proposed, the setting was identified as a technology-rich elementary classroom. Given IRB approval, I contacted school principals where I knew there were 1:1 technology classrooms. As field entry negotiations proceeded, I refined where the study actually occurred: technology-rich fourth-grade classroom.

Not all qualitative research takes place in a setting. The sample at hand used ethnographic research methods and therefore the setting was a component of the design. However, phenomenologies, for example, focus on the lived experience of a phenomena—regardless of time and place (Moustakas, 1994; Seidman, 2019; van Manen, 2014). In such cases, this part of the Anatomy should specify the parameters for selecting participants. A classic phenomenology by Moustakas (1961) asked, what is the lived experience of loneliness? The setting was not a location but an experience with a specified phenomenon, loneliness. Regardless of location or parameters of an experience, specify the setting/parameters.

Perspective: Sociocultural

Perspective (point of view) informs how you see your topic. For example, a dietician, outdoor enthusiast, chef, and parent may differ in their views of high-fat and low-carb foods. A dietician may focus on how to keep you healthy, an outdoor enthusiast may consider the weight of food while packing along the Appalachian Trail, a chef may be interested in new combinations of foods that appeal to clients, while parents may consider how to develop their children's healthy eating habits. An ant, mole, eagle, and I have varied perspectives of my front yard. An ant sees every speck of dirt to select viable options to build an ant hill, a mole values my front yard according to the grubs available, an eagle has a bird's-eye view, while I see the horrible condition of my grass or the depth of leaves that someone, other than me, should rake.

Similarly, theoretical perspectives alter how you view your topic (see Baker, 2010). In the sample question, I chose to view the *nature of literacy* from a *sociocultural perspective*. Two sociocultural tenets informed my view of literacy: (1) literacy changes as culture changes and (2) we live in a technological culture. These tenets provided the essence of my rationale: if literacy changes as culture changes and our culture is imbued with technology, then someone should examine the nature of literacy in a technological culture. That someone is me! When you craft your rationale, that someone will be you!

Some novice researchers struggle to identify their theoretical perspective(s). All research has theoretical orientations—whether the researcher is aware of them or not. Theoretical perspectives are foundational and not to be ignored for a couple of reasons. First, theoretical perspectives inform how you collect, analyze, and interpret data. A sociolinguist will collect, analyze, and interpret data differently than a cognitivist. A neurologist will collect, analyze, and interpret data differently than a sociologist. Thus, understanding your theoretical perspective can help you hone the focus of your study.

Second, you can purposely bring a new perspective to your field thereby shedding new light. For example, in my field, new light was shed when researchers examined the reading process from a cognitive perspective. Additional insights were provided during ensuing years when research examined reading from psycholinguistic and then sociocultural perspectives. Researchers continue to provide new insights by taking new perspectives toward the field. A new perspective adds dimensions to a field that previously went unnoticed. Take a new or emerging perspective and you may glean insights from your study to which previous research was blinded.

Third, you can advance the theory itself. All studies will focus on a topic and reveal insights about that topic. However, only those interested in that topic will find the research informative. Meanwhile, when your research is explicitly framed in theory, your work will inform all who share or explore your theory. While topics are domain specific, theories traverse across domains. Sociocultural theories may inform research conducted in education, medicine, business, the arts, biology, and more. In other words, while your work may inform those who examine your topic, by explicitly describing your theoretical assumptions, your work can reach across your field and permeate into other fields by extending and honing the theory itself. While you may not focus on the same substance as those in other fields, your work to advance, refine, or refute basic theoretical assumptions can impact all who consider their work from your lens(es).

I use the metaphor of table settings on a tablecloth. The plates, glasses, and silverware are likened to topics of inquiry. When you conduct research on any of these topics, your findings will inform those who also study plates, glasses, or silverware. The tablecloth is likened to the theoretical basis of your study. When you clearly articulate your theoretical perspective(s), your findings can inform everything that sits on the tablecloth. Theoretical perspectives are foundational. If your study sheds light on theoretical assumptions, then your work may inform those who share your passion for your topic, your field, as well as extend to those beyond your field. To make such impact, you must first articulate the theoretical orientation, perspective, lens, assumptions that you are making when you collect, analyze, and interpret your data.

Because my work commonly lies at the intersection of literacy and technology, I have students interested in understanding varied uses of technology (e.g., social media, virtual realities, artificial intelligence). While these technologies provide interesting fodder for understanding literacy, I propose that the lens the researcher takes toward these technologies has the potential to inform not only the intersection of literacy and technology but also anyone, within and beyond my field, who is informed by the lens I select. Theory extends beyond a topic and a field of inquiry. If your research can clarify, extend, or refute theoretical assumptions, then you are positioned to explicate the significance of your work within and beyond your field of inquiry.

Research Tradition: Ethnography

The sixth and final component of the Anatomy is the research tradition. Some common qualitative traditions are ethnography, phenomenology, case study, narrative inquiry, biography, and grounded theory, among others (see Creswell, 2017; Patton, 2014). If your work can be answered using an established tradition, then the data collection and analysis methods will be straightforward. If your work aligns with an established tradition, you already know what data you need to collect and the methods you can use to analyze them. While qualitative researchers commonly collect and analyze some combination of observation data, interviews, and/or artifacts, each tradition has distinct methods. Ethnographers collect and analyze data that are distinct from phenomenologists or narrative inquirers. While there are many ways to collect and analyze qualitative research data, traditions coalesce these methods to purposely address specific types of questions and purposely address threats to trustworthiness. There is a plethora of insightful books dedicated to expounding the data collection and analysis methods of qualitative research traditions. To dig deeper into the methods used by each tradition, see Chapter 3: *Suggested Readings*.

When I crafted the sample research question, I selected **ethnography** (research tradition designed to study culture). In order to identify and describe the characteristics of literacy in a technological setting, I needed to collect and analyze data as unobtrusively as possible. I needed to systematically account for my role in the setting. I needed to provide a thick description so the findings might be **transferable** (relatable to other settings). I therefore employed ethnographic research methods that aligned with my paradigmatic assumptions (e.g., reality is expansive, systematic analyses facilitate the ability to make estimations of reality, the researcher and researched cannot be isolated therefore researcher bias must be acknowledged, findings are contextual and therefore not generalizable but may be transferable).

PARSE THE ANATOMY

At the end of most chapters, I provide Suggested Activities that are intended to give you an opportunity to put the chapter's content into practice. When appropriate, I provide corresponding Worksheets. At the end of this chapter, I propose an activity entitled, *Parse the Anatomy* (see Suggested Activity #2 and Worksheet 1.1). Specifically, I recommend that you identify some seminal qualitative studies, preferably from your field, and identify the six parts of the Anatomy. To support your efforts, I describe a sample version of this activity. While I recommend that you identify seminal studies from your field, for two reasons, I use a sample that resides outside of my field. One, this book already has examples from my field. I want to expose you to the applicability of this book across fields. Two, if you are a new scholar, my foray into other fields may be similar to your attempts to find seminal work within your field. In other words, to emulate the efforts of novice researchers, I describe how I find a seminal study in a field where I am a novice and then describe how I identify the six parts of the Anatomy.

First, I conducted a search for "seminal" and "qualitative." If you are looking for seminal qualitative studies in your field, you will likely include your field or a specific topic to your search. I found several research reports that highlighted Quint's (1963) research as seminal for nursing. So I found Quint's article and identified the following purpose statement,

> *Focus in this article is on the viewpoint of the woman who experiences mastectomy, and attention is directed toward it as a turning point in her life. (p. 88)*

Later in the article, she states that this was an "investigation of adjustment to mastectomy" (p. 88). Similar to many qualitative reports, Quint makes purpose statements without articulating a research question. When you write your own proposal and the resulting books or articles, you too may prefer to articulate your work in terms of a purpose statement. Whether a question or purpose statement, the six components of the Anatomy remain pertinent.

Given Quint's purpose, I attempt to rephrase it as a question because this forces me to identify the primary interrogative for the study. I consider varied interrogatives. Does her purpose answer *Who, What, Where, When, Why,* or *How*? I am fairly confident that her interrogative answers *What.* She appears to ask, What are the viewpoints of women who experience mastectomy as a turning point (adjustment) in life? Now that I have her purpose converted to a question, I can parse it according to the six components of the Anatomy.

[What] are the [viewpoints] of [women who experience mastectomy] as a [turning point (adjustment) in life] ?

I turn to Worksheet 1.1 and fill out the components I ascertained thus far:

Study 1, Include reference Quint (1963)					
Paradigm	**Interrogative**	**Substance (Topic)**	**Setting/ Parameters**	**Theoretical Perspective(s)**	**Tradition**
	What	Lived experience of turning points/ adjustments	Women who have experienced a mastectomy		Something that collects and analyzes participants' viewpoints

Filling out Worksheet 1.1 forced me to differentiate between Quint's topic and the setting/parameters. I considered whether Quint's interest was on experiencing mastectomy. I dismissed this possibility because her purpose statement is about understanding a particular experience among those who had a mastectomy; her focus is on turning points/adjustments. Therefore, an inaccurate phrasing would make mastectomy the topic of this study. Instead, mastectomy is the setting/parameter of the experience she studied. As a researcher, if I parse the question inaccurately, I will spend inordinate amounts of time reviewing unrelated literature. For example, if I were Quint and thought my topic was about mastectomy, then I would have dived into mastectomy literature to discuss what is known about mastectomy and how this study contributes to the research corpus. This would result in a plethora of topics unrelated to my actual interest: turning points/adjustments.

Similarly, I was challenged to figure out where Quint's stated focus fit into the Anatomy. When Quint states that her focus is on participants' viewpoints, I wondered if viewpoints was her topic. If so, then she would have tied this work to its significance within "viewpoint" literature. She would have plunged headfirst into research about viewpoints. Given that Quint's article values the viewpoints of women who have experienced a mastectomy and the empty columns on Worksheet 1.1 are paradigm, perspective, and tradition, I considered whether Quint's stated focus fits into another part of the Anatomy. I mulled the role of viewpoints in Quint's study.

As I read Quint's article, it became obvious that viewpoints were her primary data set. Quint interviewed women who had a mastectomy to understand their turning points (adjustments). Her stated focus wasn't her topic but her data set. She collected and analyzed interview data. Not only that, but interview data were her only data set. In other words, this study did not examine cultural norms (e.g., **ethnography**), contextual data with specified parameters (e.g., **case study**), participants' stories related to turning points (e.g., **narrative inquiry**), life story from birth to present (e.g., **biography**), theories that explain the origins of turning points with the possibility of predicting the future of turning points (e.g., **grounded theory**), or collect artifacts as a primary data set (e.g., **content analysis**). When I turn to Chapter 3 and Table 3.1, by process of elimination, the remaining research tradition is phenomenology. According to Table 3.1, **phenomenology** is a research tradition designed to examine a lived experience. Bingo! Quint studied the lived experience of turning points (adjustments) among women who had a mastectomy. I can now fill out the Tradition column of Worksheet 1.1.

Given insights into Quint's interrogative, topic, setting, and research tradition, I can posit her paradigm. As stated, many journals do not ask researchers to discuss their paradigm. In fact, often this gets cut due to space limitations. When you complete Worksheet 1.1, this is the component of the Anatomy that you may have to infer. If you are reading this book as part of a graduate course, professional development, or with a group of scholars, identifying a researcher's paradigm is a great discussion point. Similar to my process for considering Quint's research tradition, I can use a process of elimination to consider her paradigm.

I turn to Chapter 2 and find Table 2.1. I explore the considerations of each paradigm. Do Quint's interrogative, topic, setting, and research tradition align with positivism, postpositivism, constructivism, critical, or post-structural considerations? I can pretty easily rule out positivism because Quint values the participants' viewpoint of their lived experiences. According to

Table 2.1, **positivism** views reality as existent regardless of human experience. Given that Quint's study is based on participants' viewpoint of their own experiences, it is likely that she was not a positivist. I look for other paradigmatic considerations that are misfits with Quint's study. **Critical paradigms** view reality as power. I see no indications that Quint examined turning points (adjustments) according to who was empowered and disempowered. I think I can rule out the critical paradigm. **Poststructural paradigms** question systematized research methods that produce tenets—especially if the tenets define reality, reify current conceptions, or produce binaries. Quint appears to conduct a systematized study in which data are coded and generate themes to represent the participants' realities. I think I can rule out poststructuralism. This leaves me with postpositivism and constructivism.

This is a perfect opportunity for me to highlight a common tendency to link research traditions to paradigms. This is most obvious when we make such statements as, if you collect numbers then you are using quantitative research methods which means you are a positivist. Conversely, we say, if you are not collecting stats, you must be doing a qualitative study because you are not a positivist. There are no direct matches between research traditions and paradigms (see Appendix B). In other words, it is possible to conduct a phenomenology as a postpositivist or a **constructivist** (paradigm that believes reality is ascribed by the human experience to the knower). Phenomenology doesn't fit in one paradigm box or the other. The same is true of ethnography, case study, narrative inquiry, biography, grounded theory, and content analysis, to mention a few. Similar actions (e.g., research methods) can be used by researchers with varied paradigms. However, the reasons for their action(s) will differ (see Chapter 2: *Introduction to Paradigms*).

While I cannot infer Quint's paradigm by her actions (e.g., research tradition), I can see how her stated focus on viewpoints aligns well with constructivism that ascribes reality to the knower. In Quint's study, she wants to understand the participants' realities. She appears to believe that reality exists within the participants. In the absence of Quint's paradigmatic explanations, I am comfortable with viewing this work as constructivistic. I could be wrong. But as I consider the insights gleaned from Quint's seminal work, one reason it appears to be seminal is that it brought constructivistic realities to nursing research.

I am now missing only one part of Worksheet 1.1: theoretical perspective(s). Unfortunately, Quint doesn't identify her theoretical perspective(s). In the 1960s, omission of theories was more common than it is today. Every field and journal is different. If you submit a research report to the best journals in my field, it will be desk rejected (not even sent to reviewers) if you omit a robust discussion of your theoretical assumptions. As described earlier in the chapter, perspective defines how you see your topic. There are differing views of food (e.g., dietician, outdoor enthusiast, chef, and parent) and my front yard (e.g., ant, mole, eagle, and me) depending on the assumptions made about food and my front yard. Likewise, given interview transcripts, Quint ascertained which comments counted as data and which comments did not count as data. Her theoretical perspective informed these decisions. I return to her article. I attempt to ascertain what theories helped Quint value some comments as representations of turning points (adjustments) but not others. When I sit back and consider the data that Quint chose to report, they include stories of heartrending angst. Her report is not statistical but coalesced around themes of fear of death, uncertain futures, and loss of agency when discussing options with surgeons.

Another strategy I use to ascertain Quint's theoretical perspective is to read through her discussion section. The discussion section highlights the significance of your study. Hopefully, your work will be significant for several reasons. It might extend the current knowledge of your topic, the theories involved, as well as paradigmatic assumptions and research methods. I chose this article because several referred to is as seminal within the field of nursing. Quint's discussion is directed toward nurses. In her discussion, Quint states, participants "have little access to nursing personnel except for brief contacts centered on procedures and physical tasks.... nursing personnel do not openly initiate discussion about mastectomy and its personal meanings is the rule, not the exception" (p. 92). Quint concludes by stating, "For nurses to accept responsibility in this problem, however, they must be willing to forego the practice of saying, 'That's the doctor's responsibility'" (p. 92). The discussion highlights the trauma the participants endured and how nurses do not have the opportunity to discuss the trauma and support women who have gone through a mastectomy. While I lack knowledge of theoretical perspectives invoked in nursing, I can make some broad inferences. In a general sense, it seems to me that Quint relies on theories of self-esteem, fear, and agency in order to collect, analyze, and discuss her data. She is not invoking theories related to chemistry or biology. Rather, she seems to feature the psychology of experiencing trauma and how nurses are needed to support women who undergo mastectomy. Unfortunately, Quint's article omits how her work relates to theories and how it pushes theories and possibly the field of nursing forward. Nonetheless, when I consider broad fields of inquiry (e.g., psychology, chemistry, biology) I can see where her work fits. To complete Worksheet 1.1, I therefore specify fields of inquiry all the while acknowledging the actual theories remain indistinct.

Study 1, Include reference Quint (1963)					
Paradigm	**Interrogative**	**Substance (Topic)**	**Setting/ Parameters**	**Theoretical Perspective(s)**	**Tradition**
Constructivist	What	Lived experience of turning points/ adjustments	Women who have experienced a mastectomy	Derived from psychology	Pheno-menology

I completed Worksheet 1.1 with a pretty good estimation of the six components of the Anatomy of a seminal study. I have to admit, while completing this Suggested Activity, I wondered, Why am I doing this? What's the value of this Suggested Activity? I return to the Introduction of this book which states,

> *The essence of research design resides in your ability to articulate research questions. The research question is the progenitor of the study. A well-crafted question embodies all the design elements for your study thereby providing the skeletal structure of your research design. Ask a well-crafted question and the design will fall into place.*

The purpose of this book is to provide a heuristic that researchers can readily invoke to formulate robust, viable research questions that encapsulate the design elements you need to conduct qualitative research. Given a robust research question, in which the researcher can parse the components of the Anatomy, you will save time, energy, and resources. In Quint's example, if she had inaccurately parsed her study by identifying a different interrogative, topic, setting, research tradition, paradigm, or theoretical perspective(s), then her study would have been a different study. Of course, a different study may have been seminal too. But it wouldn't have accomplished her stated focus. It is my hope that the heuristic invoked in this book will help you clarify and articulate your research interests in such a way as to give you the ability to adroitly design and conduct research.

While completing Worksheet 1.1, I also wondered if only proficient qualitative researchers could possibly fill out Worksheet 1.1. After all, I had to skip ahead to Chapter 3, Table 3.1, Chapter 2, and Table 2.1 to complete the Suggested Activity. How can novices possibly know to do this? The short answer is, they can't. Filling out Worksheet 1.1 may be like reading an unknown foreign language. That's OK. I propose that this activity allows you to get your proverbial feet wet. It gives you the opportunity to know what you do and don't know. You may know more than you think you do. By wrestling to complete Worksheet 1.1 you can personalize this book. You can start to build bridges from the content in this book to your research. It has been argued that learning is spiral instead of linear. In which case, anytime you formulate a new research agenda, you may find it helpful to return to this book and once again clarify your thought to ask viable and robust research questions that target your substantive passions. Discussing Worksheet 1.1 with others may help you ascertain what you know, want to know, and how the Anatomy can inform your work. So, I agree: Worksheet 1.1 may be overwhelming. Give it your best shot and then turn to Chapters 2–5 to develop proficiencies that will put you in good stead to design and conduct qualitative studies as well as provide feedback to qualitative researchers.

CHAPTER SUMMARY

In summary, based on decades of designing qualitative research with doctoral students and colleagues, I honed a heuristic that can be used to facilitate the design of qualitative research. This heuristic is based on the Anatomy of a Qualitative Research Question that consists of six components:

1. Paradigm
2. Interrogative
3. Substance (topic)
4. Setting/Parameters
5. Perspective
6. Research tradition

To help you become familiar with each component of the Anatomy, I deconstructed a sample research question. I described how the paradigm, interrogative, topic, setting, theoretical perspective, and research tradition informed the construction of the sample research question. Next, I encouraged you to practice using your newfound knowledge by identifying the parts of the Anatomy in a seminal study. To support your efforts, I modeled how I went about finding each component in a seminal qualitative study.

Now that I have introduced you to the Anatomy, deconstructed a sample question, and identified each component of the Anatomy in a seminal study, I proceed to Chapter 2 and the beginning point of research design: your paradigm.

SUGGESTED ACTIVITIES AND DISCUSSIONS

1. Write your overarching research question using all six parts of the Anatomy: paradigm, interrogative, substance/topic, setting, perspective, research tradition. In Chapter 3, we will discuss strategies to hone your question.
2. Go to Worksheet 1.1. Identify 3–5 seminal qualitative research studies in your field. Identify the six parts of the Anatomy for each study. Discuss your identification with others. Based on your identification and discussion, revise your research question.

WORKSHEET 1.1 ■ Parse the Anatomy

Identify 3–5 seminal qualitative research studies in your field. Identify the six parts of the Anatomy for each study. If you are unable to identify any of the parts, leave it blank. Discuss your identification and blanks with others. Based on your discussion, consider your own research question.

Study 1, Include reference

Paradigm	Interrogative	Substance (Topic)	Setting/Parameters	Theoretical Perspective(s)	Tradition

Study 2, Include reference

Paradigm	Interrogative	Substance (Topic)	Setting/Parameters	Theoretical Perspective(s)	Tradition

(Continued)

WORKSHEET 1.1 ■ Parse the Anatomy (Continued)

Study 3, Include reference

Paradigm	Interrogative	Substance (Topic)	Setting/Parameters	Theoretical Perspective(s)	Tradition

Study 4, Include reference

Paradigm	Interrogative	Substance (Topic)	Setting/Parameters	Theoretical Perspective(s)	Tradition

Study 5, Include reference

Paradigm	Interrogative	Substance (Topic)	Setting/Parameters	Theoretical Perspective(s)	Tradition

2 THE ROLE OF PARADIGMS IN RESEARCH DESIGN

CHAPTER OUTLINE

I commonly hear people repeat what is apparently a widespread adage:

> *You don't begin research design by deciding whether to do quantitative or qualitative research. You ask a research question and then employ the research methods that will answer your question.*

While I agree with this statement, I contend that it is misleading. Research design doesn't begin with the question. I propose that research design begins with your worldview, your paradigm. This is why I identify paradigm as the first component of the Anatomy. I commonly ask my doctoral students, why do we conduct research? I receive several answers. Some say to learn new information, or gain new insights, or contribute to current conceptions. I echo Lincoln and Guba (1985a) and argue that we conduct research to grapple with truth and to make sense of reality. Your beliefs about truth and reality formulate your paradigm.

Throughout this book, I argue that you will be empowered to make informed research design decisions when you make your tacit assumptions explicit. This is true of your paradigm, theoretical perspectives, research traditions, data collection and analysis methods, and the genre of your research report. When you make the tacit explicit, you are empowered to recognize how your work aligns with other researchers. We all want to believe we are inventing the wheel. We like to think, no one has been so clever as to ask the questions we ask, use the methods we use, and write the report that we write. I hope your work is significant and changes the world. I propose that one strategy for designing impactful research is to unpack your assumptions, compare them with the assumptions made by others, and explicate how your work moves current assumptions forward. In so doing, you can compare your work to the work that has already been done. You are empowered to discuss the significance of your work. When you leave your assumptions implied you set yourself up for drowning in a sea of insights that make it difficult to articulate their significance.

Begin your research design by recognizing your basic paradigmatic assumptions. You ask the questions that you ask because of your view of reality. Whether you are aware of it or not, your research questions emanate from your paradigm. Because research design doesn't begin with your question but with your view of reality, I begin the exploration of the Anatomy and structure the sample question with a brief explication of research paradigms.

INTRODUCTION TO PARADIGMS

Hatch (2002) described research paradigms as the confluence of ontology, epistemology, **methodology** (the philosophy and corresponding methods used to conduct a study), and report genre (see Appendix B). The categorization of paradigms differs across theorists and remains organic and fluid. For example, in 1994 Guba and Lincoln described four paradigms: positivism, post-positivism, critical, and constructivism. In 2005, they added participatory as a paradigm (Lincoln & Guba). Denzin and Lincoln (2005) described four paradigms: positivism, postpositivism, constructivism-interpretivism, and critical. By 2018, Denzin and Lincoln parsed five paradigms: positivist/postpositivist, critical, feminist, constructivist/interpretivist, and participatory/postmodern/poststructural. Others echo positivism, postpositivism, and constructivism and then elaborate on transformative, emancipatory, postcolonial, and indigenous paradigms (Chilisa, 2011). Yet others describe positivism, postpositivism, constructivism, and critical while including pragmatism (Morgan, 2014). Regardless of how you slice and label the pie, or even believe the pie exists, your paradigm influences what research questions you deem to be worth asking. For the purposes of this book, I will slice and label the paradigm pie by highlighting positivism, postpositivism, critical, constructivism, and poststructuralism (see Table 2.1).

TABLE 2.1 ■ Paradigms: Considerations, Historical Roots, and Related Scholars

Paradigms	Considerations	Historical Roots	Related Scholars
Positivism	Reality exists regardless of human experience; systematic methods can reveal reality; the researcher and researched can be isolated; findings are generalizable	Natural Sciences Psychology Scientific Method Sociology	Comte Durkheim Pavlov Skinner Watson
Postpositivism	Reality is expansive; systematic analyses facilitate the ability to make estimations of reality; the researcher and researched cannot be isolated therefore researcher bias must be acknowledged; findings are contextual and therefore not generalizable but may be transferable	Philosophy Social Sciences Sociology	Kuhn Popper
Constructivism	Reality is ascribed by the human experience; reality is individually invented while socially negotiated	Education Hermeneutics Linguistics Philosophy Postmodernism Cognitive Psychology Sociology	Bakhtin Husserl Piaget Ernst von Glasersfeld Vygotsky
Critical	Reality is power; existence is political; research is an emancipatory act that demands change	Humanities Liberation Theology Literary Criticism Social Sciences	Baudrillard Chomsky Foucault Freire Horkheimer Marx
Poststructural	Reality is plural and fluid; reality may be	Linguistics Literary Theory	Barthes Deleuze

(Continued)

TABLE 2.1 ■ Paradigms: Considerations, Historical Roots, and Related Scholars (Continued)

Paradigms	Considerations	Historical Roots	Related Scholars
	chaotic and illogical; concepts of reality must be interrogated for reification and binaries; at its core, knowledge is limited and instable	Philosophy Sociology	Derrida Eco Kristeva Lyotard

Note: Table 2.1 provides a mere gist of paradigms and is in danger of misrepresenting these expansive concepts. Across and within paradigms, there is a range of considerations, historical roots, and scholars. To deepen your understanding, be sure to delve into the intricacies across and within paradigms.

Identifying your paradigmatic assumptions will help you articulate your research questions. Instead of starting your research design with your question, I encourage you to begin with unpacking your paradigmatic assumptions. Table 2.1 provides some general distinctions. However, I want to point out that these distinctions are simplistic and should be valued accordingly. When you dig deeper into paradigmatic assumptions, you will find "blurred" (Geertz, 1993; Lincoln & Guba, 2005) rather than clearly boxed considerations.

In a basic sense, ontology is the philosophy of existence. Consider Descartes' (1637) argument for reality, *I think therefore I am*, as an example of an ontological statement. Your ontological assumptions will influence what questions you consider to be worth asking. For positivists, existence is external to human beliefs, waiting to be discovered. Research can be designed to isolate variables and examine existence. Nonpositivists view existence as a flexible reality. Some contend existence is too expansive to grasp (postpositivism), created by those who experience it (constructivism), centered on power (critical), as well as reified and therefore conceptualizations of existence are questionable (poststructuralism).

Similarly, your epistemological assumptions inform your research questions. In brief, epistemology is the philosophy of the existence of knowledge. Positivism views knowledge as preexistent and independent of knowers. Postpositivism acknowledges that the researcher and the researched are inseparable therefore bias can and must be acknowledged. In my field of education, the 1990s constructivist revolution epitomized epistemological enlightenment (e.g., Steffe & Gale, 1995). Constructivists helped my field to examine the epistemological assumptions made in education. How does knowledge exist? Constructivists argued, knowledge is formulated by the knower. Critical epistemologies contend that knowledge exists as power. Research is therefore an emancipatory act that inherently requires change. Poststructuralists question assumptions made about the existence of knowledge and posit that knowledge as known is questionable.

Paradigms are similar to religious views in this sense: they do not change for the sake of a study. Paradigms are deeply held convictions that explain reality. You change paradigms with the regularity you change religions (i.e., not very often). It is possible to change paradigms—but it is a life-changing event. I propose that you have paradigmatic views of reality—whether you know it or not. With the warning that the paradigm descriptions I provide merely scratch the surface, I pose the following considerations to assist you in your pursuit of understanding your own paradigmatic assumptions. Do you believe reality exists—regardless of whether humans ever walked the earth? You might be a positivist. Do you believe reality exists—but is so inconceivably expansive that we can only make sense of our immediate realities? You might be a postpositivist. Do you believe reality is subjective because it is individually invented while socially negotiated? You might be a constructivist. Do you believe that the essence of reality is power and the purpose of research is to enact change? You might be a criticalist. Do you believe that concepts of reality are reified and questionable? (In fact, the notion of paradigms rubs you wrong.) You might be a poststructuralist. Examining your paradigmatic assumptions will help you hone your research question. Begin research design by asking questions that examine reality. You will likely find research that asks questions aligned to your paradigm ring true while those misaligned ring hollow. Ask research questions that help you make sense of reality by first identifying and understanding your paradigmatic assumptions about reality.

If you tend to ask cause/effect/impact questions, you might be a positivist. On the other hand, if you are a nonpositivist but find yourself asking cause/effect/impact questions, you need to consider ways to rephrase your question. I find that many novice researchers commonly ask cause/effect/impact questions but do not see their ontological or epistemological beliefs represented in positivism. I wonder if our culture, steeped in the scientific method, influences us to consider reality in cause/effect/impact terms. Maybe you are a positivist and cause/effect/impact questions are meaningful to you. That's great! You can formulate a corresponding research design. However, if you are a nonpositivist, peruse the literature in your field and find varied ways to formulate research questions that grapple with nonpositivistic realities.

Otherwise, you may ask research questions that precipitate research methods and findings that you find vapid.

RESEARCH DESIGN AND THE ROLE OF PARADIGMS

Finding My Paradigm: Process of Elimination

To demonstrate how you might think through your own paradigm, I return to the sample question,

> *Given a postpositivist paradigm, what is the nature of literacy in a technology-rich fourth-grade classroom from a sociocultural perspective using ethnographic research methods?*

In order to articulate my dissertation question, I examined my paradigmatic assumptions. Some of this discovery was a process of elimination. I knew that I was not a positivist. While positivism may make sense in the natural sciences, I could not reconcile it with social sciences. Before becoming a professor, I was a classroom teacher who was required to implement end-of-year standardized state-wide tests that were derived from positivistic views of reality. I viewed these assessments as disingenuous and invalid. My reaction to standardized state tests was a good indication that I was not a positivist.

During my graduate studies, constructivism was all the rage. I wanted to fit in but eventually recognized that paradigmatically I am a postpositivist. A tenet of constructivism is that reality is ascribed by the human experience. However, I believe that reality may exist apart from human existence. I therefore continued to examine my own paradigmatic assumptions. A tenet of the critical paradigm is that reality is power. I am so thankful that critical theorists exist as I am in constant need to interrogate my own reification of empowerment and disempowerment. While I value the insights and challenges provided by my critical colleagues, I do not walk into a room and view the situation in terms of who is empowered and disempowered. Thus, I recognized that I am not paradigmatically critical. Similarly, I value the insights provided by my poststructuralist colleagues. I especially value being challenged to question binaries. Nonetheless, this is not my gut ontological or epistemological orientation. Whether I like it or not, I currently view reality as a postpositivist who sees ontology and epistemology as complicated, complex, beyond human purveyance while possibly existing without humanity.

Paradigmatic Implications: Recapitulating a Sample Question

My paradigm has implications for what I view as viable strategies for making sense of reality—my research methods. For example, as a post-positivist, I am interested in the interconnectedness of reality and therefore cannot claim to separate my role in data collection and analysis from the setting (positivism) but must systematically account for my role as well as articulate my assumptions/biases. My data collection and analyses are systematic so I can attempt to make estimations of reality. Because I believe that reality is not generalizable (positivism) but may be transferable, I collect data in natural settings and attempt to provide thick descriptions of these settings so that my readers can transfer insights to their own settings.

To help you explore paradigms and consider implications for your study, I recapitulate my dissertation question according to varied paradigms. These are simplistic, rudimentary, broad stroke recapitulations intended to help you consider the implications of paradigms when you formulate research questions. These are mere possibilities. I begin with positivism. How might a positivist rephrase the sample research question? A positivist believes that reality exists regardless of human experience and the researcher and researched can be isolated. As such, reality is best ascertained by isolating and measuring variables. If I were a positivist, I might ask,

> *Given a positivist paradigm, what impact does word processing have on fourth-graders' organization of paragraphs from a behavioral perspective using TOWE (Test of Written Expression)?*

The paradigmatic shift has implications for all parts of the question (see Table 2.2). The topic shifts from the *nature of literacy* to the *impact of word processing* on a variable (e.g., organization of paragraphs) that can be measured using psychometrics that have established validity and reliability (e.g., TOWE). As posed, the setting can be anywhere the participants can take the TOWE test. The focus of this study would be on pre–post measures, not on the social norms of a classroom. In fact, the way this question is framed, word processing may not occur in a classroom setting. To conduct this study, I would need to set the parameters for what is meant by word processing (e.g., 20-minutes 3 days/week for 3 months in a project lab, other) and those who meet the parameters would be viable participants. Sociocultural theory provides few insights into the results of the *TOWE* test. Therefore, other perspective(s) are needed to interpret the findings. In this case, I chose to ground my interpretation of results in behaviorism.

TABLE 2.2 ■ Sample Question: Exploring Paradigmatic Implications

	Postpositivism	Positivism	Constructivism	Critical	Poststructural
Interrogative	What	What	How	Who	What
Topic	Nature of literacy	Impact on paragraph organization	Make meaning of and with digital texts	Empowered to communicate	Binaries
Setting	Technology-rich fourth-grade classroom	Location where test can be given	Technology-rich fourth-grade classroom	Technology-rich fourth-grade classroom	Concepts of the nature of literacy
Tradition	Ethnography	Quantitative, *TOWE* pre–post test	Case study	Case study	Metatheory
Perspective	Sociocultural	Behavioral	Social learning theory	Feminist Theory	Deconstructive

A constructivist might believe, among other tenets, that reality is ascribed by the human experience and created by those who experience it, and knowledge is formulated by the knower. This view of reality has implications for how the sample question would be formulated. If I were a constructivist, I might ask,

> *Given a constructivist paradigm, how do fourth-graders in a technology-rich classroom make meaning of and with digital texts from a social learning theory perspective using case study methods?*

The topic shifts from the *nature of literacy* to *how meaning is made*. In other words, the postpositivist's study identifies *characteristics of literacy* while the constructivist's study examines the *process of making meaning*. Both may conduct their studies in a technology-rich fourth-grade classroom. Sociocultural theory may help the constructivist understand the findings but in this case I chose to leverage social learning theory.

A critical researcher views reality in terms of power, life as inherently political, and that the purpose of research is emancipatory. The sample research question may become,

> *Given a critical paradigm, who is dis/empowered to communicate in a technology-rich fourth-grade classroom from a feminist perspective using case study methods?*

The focus shifts from the *nature of literacy* to *dis/empowerment*. The setting may remain the same but the perspective will likely shift to theories that help the researcher examine dis/empowerment. In this case, I specified feminist theory. The findings will be used to exact change to current cultural practices. The research tradition, ethnography, might remain the same but case study may allow increased flexibility to focus on dis/empowerment.

A poststructuralist believes that reality is plural and fluid, it may be chaotic and illogical and concepts of reality must be interrogated for reification and binaries. The sample research question might become,

> *Given a poststructuralist paradigm, what binaries constitute the nature of literacy in a technology-rich fourth-grade classroom from a deconstructive perspective using metatheory?*

It is a reach to rephrase the sample question as a poststructuralist because a poststructuralist may reject the notion of a research question and the structure of a research tradition. The notion of paradigms may be deemed as an example of paradigmatic fallacy. Rephrasing the sample question in post-structural terms may be questionable because doing so maintains previously held structural views of reality. Nonetheless, for the sake of juxtaposition, I pose that the focus of a poststructural study might interrogate binaries leveraged in literacy studies (e.g., read and write, decode and encode, printed text and digital text). The setting might remain the same but the focus might question previously held concepts of literacy. Sociocultural theory would provide few insights while deconstructive theories might be useful. Systematic data collection and analysis may reify illusions of reality. Using metatheory, the goal would be to examine previously held conceptions of the nature of literacy.

Proposals and Reports: Placement of Paradigm

When you write a proposal or research report, you will likely discuss your paradigm in the opening paragraph/section of your methodology—not to be confused with your related literature (see Table 5.2 and Table 5.3). Use your paradigmatic assumptions as the framework for your methodological rationale. When reviewers (e.g., doctoral committee members, journal articles, funding agencies) determine the quality of a study, they commonly examine whether the paradigmatic assumptions are a good fit with the research methods. If you are a positivist but fail to isolate variables, your research design may be questionable. If you are a constructivist but collect pre and post data without accounting for how *being* and *knowledge* were ascribed by the participants, your research design may be questionable. If you are a critical theorist but describe phenomena as if they are void of power and lack requisite emancipatory actions, your research design may be questionable. Take the time to examine your paradigmatic assumptions. Such efforts allow you to pursue your understanding of ontology and epistemology in methodologically viable ways.

UNVEIL YOUR PARADIGMATIC ASSUMPTIONS: ASK RESEARCH QUESTIONS

Novice and experienced researchers wrestle with understanding their paradigmatic views of reality. I want to point out the reflexive relationship between paradigmatic worldviews and research questions. I find that asking questions can help you examine your paradigmatic assumptions. In other words, I do not want to imply that you must grasp your paradigm before you start asking questions. In fact, asking questions may help to unveil your paradigm. I encourage you to purposely frame your question from different paradigms. How would you ask your question if you were a positivist? postpositivist? constructivist? criticalist? poststructuralist? other? A challenge you may encounter is that when you read research reports, the paradigm is often implied and not explicitly stated. It can be difficult, therefore, to gather sample research questions according to paradigm so you can make comparisons. Whether stated or not, all questions are rooted in paradigmatic assumptions. Select some of the seminal studies in your field and see if you can determine the paradigmatic assumptions that are inherent to the questions they pose. Do you esteem some research over other research? Maybe you share paradigmatic assumptions with the researchers who conducted the study.

CHAPTER SUMMARY

When using the Anatomy to formulate a research question, begin with an explicit statement of your paradigm (worldview). Research questions are inherently derived from paradigmatic assumptions. You can waste time, energy, and resources if you ignore your own paradigmatic worldview. Take the time to begin or refine your foray into paradigms. Identify and discuss the paradigmatic assumptions embedded in 3–5 seminal studies in your field. Reformulate your own research question based on varied paradigmatic assumptions. Understanding your paradigm will empower you to articulate and refine your research question. Recapitulating your question situated within different paradigms may help you realize your beliefs about reality. We conduct research to make sense of reality. To avoid vapid research, formulate research questions and conduct studies that help you make sense of reality.

SUGGESTED ACTIVITIES AND DISCUSSIONS

1. Formulate a simple question (e.g., what do I want for dinner?) and attempt to reformulate the question according to paradigm. How would a positivist ask about dinner? postpositivist? constructivist? criticalist? poststructuralist?
2. Select seminal research reports in your field. Can you ascertain the paradigmatic assumptions inherent to the overarching research question? Discuss why you assign varied paradigms to a range of studies.
3. Given the propensity of our culture to ask cause/effect/impact questions, which assumes a positivist paradigm, can you translate some cause/effect/impact questions into nonpositivistic language? For example, how would you translate

this question across paradigms: What is the impact of social media on parental interactions with their children?

4. I find that Social Science doctoral students commonly appreciate the opportunity to examine pragmatism as a paradigm. The essence of pragmatism is to consider "what works." If this consideration resonates with you, one way to begin this exploration is to read and discuss Morgan (2014).

SUGGESTED READINGS

Hatch, J. A. (2002). Deciding to do a qualitative study. In *Doing qualitative research in education settings* (pp. 1–35). Albany, NY: State University of New York Press.

Kivunja, C., & Kuyini, A. B. (2017). Understanding and applying research paradigms in educational contexts. *International Journal of Higher Education*, 6(5), 26–41.

Lincoln, Y. S., Lynham, S. A., & Guba, E. G. (2018). Paradigmatic controversies, contradictions, and emerging confluences, revisited. In N. K. Denzin, & Y. S. Lincoln (Eds.), *The Sage handbook of qualitative research* (5th ed., pp. 108–150). Thousand Oaks, CA: SAGE.

Morgan, D. L. (2014). Pragmatism as a paradigm for social research. *Qualitative Inquiry*, 20(8), 1045–1053. doi: 10.1177/1077800413513733

Williams, J. (2014). *Understanding poststructuralism*. New York, NY: Routledge.

3 USING METACOGNITIVE STRATEGIES TO BRING THE ANATOMY TO LIFE

CHAPTER OUTLINE

In Chapter 1, I broke down a sample qualitative research question into six parts and described those parts as the Anatomy of a Qualitative Research Question. Chapter 1 was portrayed as the puzzle box top: an overview of the big picture by defining each part of the Anatomy. In Chapter 2, I argued that research emanates from your worldview, your paradigm. Now that you have been introduced to the Anatomy and considered the role of your worldview, the question remains: how do you translate your topic into a research question? In this chapter, I proceed to the pieces of the puzzle by describing metacognitive strategies you can use to transform your topic into a fully functioning, design imbued, research question.

Cognition is rapid, messy, complex, and difficult to describe. To bring the Anatomy to life, I propose metacognitive strategies that you can use while you brainstorm, draft, brainstorm some more, refine, and design qualitative studies. When students come to me with a topic, I find that I consistently invoke the parts of the Anatomy (see Chapter 1) but quickly proceed to the following strategies to move from an idea to a question—or several potential questions.

One metacognitive strategy is to make substitutions. I change the interrogative, tradition, setting, and perspective. Another strategy is to ponder hypothetical answers. Yet another is to rephrase the question in terms of the final report's genre. In addition, I revisit paradigmatic assumptions. In other words, I simultaneously consider:

- **varied substitutions**,
- **corresponding findings**, as well as
- implications for the **report genre**, and
- **paradigmatic assumptions**.

When formulating and reformulating research questions, I skip around. I've heard it said that Michelangelo was able to produce seminal sculptures of the human anatomy (e.g., The David) by chipping away from blocks of stone anything that didn't resemble what he was sculpting. Like a sculptor with a chisel, I chip away at the idea with these strategies until I formulate a research question that cuts to the chase of what I want to examine. In this chapter, I tackle each strategy: one at a time. I attempt to slow down the complex and instantaneous cognitive processes used to refine a research question. One danger is that readers may infer this as a step-by-step guide. Instead, consider this chapter to be a description of cognitive strategies that might be used to formulate a qualitative research question that embodies a corresponding research design. In reality, these strategies are instantaneous, simultaneous, and recursive. In Chapter 4, I situate these metacognitive strategies within composite conversations that I commonly have with doctoral students and colleagues as we revise and formulate overarching qualitative research questions.

MAKE SUBSTITUTIONS

In Chapter 2, I made substitutions to my paradigm and discussed corresponding implications for the other parts of the Anatomy. In this section, I return to the sample question and continue with the metacognitive strategy of making substitutions. I pick up the process with the interrogative, topic, setting, and tradition.

Substitute the Interrogative

Consider the interrogative. Whether you ask *Who, What, Where, When, Why,* or *How* will change the course of your study. In the stated sample, the study would radically change course if I made the following substitutions:

> *Who is the nature of literacy…*
>
> *Where is the nature of literacy…*
>
> *When is the nature of literacy…*
>
> *Why is the nature of literacy…*
>
> *How is the nature of literacy…*

In this section, I explore implications of substituting *What* for other interrogatives. The sample question is:

> *Given a postpositivist paradigm, ~~what is the nature of literacy~~ in a technology-rich fourth-grade classroom from a sociocultural perspective using ethnographic research methods?*

Most interrogative substitutions create grammatical gaffes and require revisions to the topic. For example, *Who* is the nature of literacy, *Where* is the nature of literacy, *When* is the nature of literacy, *Why* is the nature of literacy, and *How* is the nature of literacy are nonsensical and require refined foci. Specifically, *Who* is the nature of literacy might become:

> *Given a postpositivist paradigm, ~~what is the nature of literacy~~ [who reads and writes] in a technology-rich fourth-grade classroom from a sociocultural perspective using ethnographic research methods?*

Given a revised interrogative, I can critique the substitution and consider whether it hones or distracts from the essence of my query. I hypothetically answer my question with each interrogative and evaluate whether the answers cut to the core of my inquiry. In this sample, hypothetical answers to *Who reads and writes* in this setting might be Sally, Johnny, and likely most or all of the students in this classroom. A list of the students in this class is not a very intriguing answer. I move to another interrogative.

Given a postpositivist paradigm, ~~what~~ [where] is the nature of literacy in a technology-rich fourth-grade classroom from a sociocultural perspective using ethnographic research methods?

Where is the nature of literacy is nonsensical. The topic needs to shift. For example, it may make grammatical sense to ask:

Given a postpositivist paradigm, ~~what~~ [where] is ~~the nature of~~ literacy in a technology-rich fourth-grade classroom from a sociocultural perspective using ethnographic research methods?

The potential answers require operationalizing my topic: literacy. If the study is focused on finding where literacy occurs in this technology-rich classroom, the question should specify what I am looking for when I claim to find the location of literacy. I could specify:

Given a postpositivist paradigm, ~~what~~ [where] ~~is the nature of literacy~~ [do students read alphabetic text] in a technology-rich fourth-grade classroom from a sociocultural perspective using ethnographic research methods?

Hypothetical answers include: at their desks, in the reading center, in the computer center, or at the school library. Maybe the question needs to be further honed. Because literacy commonly involves reading and writing alphabetic text, maybe the question is not about where the students reside but where the alphabetic text resides. In this case, the question might be:

Given a postpositivist paradigm, ~~what~~ [where] ~~is the nature of literacy~~ [does alphabetic text reside] in a technology-rich fourth-grade classroom from a sociocultural perspective using ethnographic research methods?

Hypothetical answers might be that the alphabetic text resides in books, magazines, eReaders, and computers. For my purposes, these hypothetical answers ring hollow. I move to another interrogative:

Given a postpositivist paradigm, ~~what~~ [when] is the nature of literacy in a technology-rich fourth-grade classroom from a sociocultural perspective using ethnographic research methods?

Similar to other interrogative substitutions, *When* is the nature of literacy requires grammatical revisions. Maybe I could ask:

> *Given a postpositivist paradigm, ~~what is the nature of literacy~~ [when do fourth-graders] in a technology-rich ~~fourth-grade~~ classroom [use technology to read and write] from a sociocultural perspective using ethnographic research methods?*

These revisions remain awkward but I can still hypothesize and critique possible answers. For example, answers to this question might include: when the teacher requires them to use technology, during free time, when they are not allowed (e.g., text their friends when they should be completing non-technology assignments). For my purposes, these hypothetical answers miss the mark. Therefore, for this study, framing the overarching research question in terms of *When* is lackluster.

So far, I have explored the implications of asking *Who, What, Where,* and *When*. I proceed to asking *Why*.

> *Given a postpositivist paradigm, ~~what~~ [why] is the nature of literacy in a technology-rich fourth-grade classroom from a sociocultural perspective using ethnographic research methods?*

Why is the nature of literacy is an incomplete question. By asking why, I need to insert a characteristic of literacy. I would need to revisit related literature to identify viable characteristics. For the sake of examining the potential of asking *why*, I will temporarily insert a characteristic derived from related literature: multimodal.

> *Given a postpositivist paradigm, ~~what~~ [why] is the nature of literacy [multimodal] in a technology-rich fourth-grade classroom from a sociocultural perspective using ethnographic research methods?*

Arguably, ethnographic research methods may not reveal why literacy is multimodal in this setting. In fact, it may not be multimodal. If I want to understand the multimodal nature of literacy, I might do better to shift my research methods. In the next section, I explore the affordances of substituting varied traditions. For the sake of examining the utility of a *why* question, I will nonetheless posit answers. Maybe literacy is multimodal because the teacher requires students to incorporate illustrations, video, sound effects, music, and voice-overs anytime they use technology to read or write. Maybe literacy is multimodal because the students brought multimodal skills with them to the classroom and had access to technology that allowed them to read and write multiple modes.

What if I ask, *How*?

> *Given a postpositivist paradigm, ~~what~~ [how] is the nature of literacy in a technology-rich fourth-grade classroom from a sociocultural perspective using ethnographic research methods?*

Again, the question is incomplete and requires a topical revision. What if I stick with the notion of multimodality?

> *Given a postpositivist paradigm, ~~what~~ [how] is ~~the nature of~~ literacy [multimodal] in a technology-rich fourth-grade classroom from a sociocultural perspective using ethnographic research methods?*

Possible answers might generate *the process* by which literacy is multimodal. In other words, the focus of a *How* question might be to identify a list of steps. How is literacy multimodal? First, students select YouTube to explore a topic. Next, students watch videos, etc. Do you want to conduct a study that finds the process of becoming? Then asking *How* questions may be useful to you. Alternatively, asking *How* may not focus on a process but a description. *How* is the nature of literacy multimodal might be the same as *In what ways* is literacy multimodal? Potential answers might include: literacy in this setting includes reading (making sense of) video, sound effects, voice-overs, music, illustrations, animations, photography, and graphs. Because *How* can imply both a process and a list of characteristics, I encourage researchers to clarify their focus for themselves and their audience. The rationale and related literature will shift depending on the focus of *How*.

When I refer to the interrogative as part of the Anatomy of a Qualitative Research Question, I am not referring to questions that researchers pursue along the way. Rather, each component of the Anatomy refers to parts of the overarching research query; the purpose of the study. I make this point because in a general sense, when *Who* and *When* are used to frame the overarching research question, they may imply a survey or descriptive statistics methods. I am sure that there are exceptions so I am unwilling to make an outright statement that claims all qualitative researchers should avoid *Who* and *When* to frame their research. In fact, *Who* and *When* are significant components of many qualitative studies. For example, ethnographic studies seek to understand *Who* and *When* to ultimately make sense of the culture being studied. In other words, *Who* and *When* are subquestions that are key to understanding the overarching research question. When I refer to substituting the interrogative, I am referring to the overarching research question—not the subquestions.

Play with varied interrogatives and unearth the potential of each for your own work. The interrogative is like a rudder. It helps to steer your study. Be sure you steer according to where you want to go. It is worth considering which interrogative directs your query in the right direction.

Substitute the Research Tradition

When I was in graduate school, I was assigned an article to read that talked about different qualitative research traditions. A light bulb went off! I had not realized that there were different kinds (traditions) of qualitative studies. In the ensuing years, books have been written that compare traditions (e.g., Creswell, 2017; Patton, 2014) as well as explicate the ins and outs of specific traditions (e.g., ethnography, case study, narrative inquiry). You may be unfamiliar with varied traditions. Using the sample research question, in this section, I browse through a series of tradition substitutions. I highlight common foci of each tradition and a few corresponding implications. The goal is for you to glean sufficient insights so that you can identify traditions that may be useful to advancing your study and proceed to resources that help you proficiently employ corresponding research methods (see Chapter 3: *Suggested Readings*).

There are varied uses of the terms *research tradition* and *methods*. In particular, some use tradition and methods interchangeably. I do not. To me, these are different constructs. Throughout this book, when I refer to research tradition or simply tradition, I am referring to a group of data collection and analysis procedures (methods) that purposely coalesce to address threats to trustworthiness. I differentiate traditions from methods because research methods are simply that: a method for collecting or analyzing data. In other words, a method is similar to following a recipe with specified ingredients (e.g., observations, interviews, artifacts) and steps. If I persist with the cooking metaphor, a tradition is similar to frying, baking, grilling, or sous vide. All traditions use similar ingredients but for different reasons and with varied methods. For example, the methods used to conduct ethnographic interviews differ from those used to conduct phenomenological interviews. These differences hinge on how the data sets (e.g., observations, interviews, artifact) work together to strategically offset, as much as possible, threats to trustworthiness. Throughout this book, tradition refers to a cohesive orchestration of methods used to conduct a particular study to answer the research question while mitigating threats to trustworthiness.

The distinctions between tradition and methods grow blurry when a tradition relies heavily on one type of data. For example, content analysis studies predominantly collect and analyze artifact data. The methods for conducting a content analysis *study* are more robust than using content analysis *methods* as part of another tradition. Understandably, confusion arises because our current vernacular lacks distinctions between content analysis as a tradition and method. Throughout this section, I attempt to demonstrate how substituting your tradition can help you refine your research question. After you narrow down your best guesses for a research tradition that supports your work, I encourage you to dive deeper into the methods used by tapping into books and resources that focus on specific traditions (see Chapter 3: *Suggested Readings*).

Be aware that not all research questions have a research tradition that is a good fit. In fact, the inadequacies of current research traditions to answer proposed questions are the genesis of new research traditions. Qualitative research methods have evolved for centuries and continue to evolve when researchers expound the inadequacies of traditions and corresponding methods. So, if the current vanguard of qualitative research traditions falls short of giving you the data collection and analysis methods that you need to answer your question while supporting trustworthiness, it may be time to propose an amalgamation of current traditions or create new strategies. Given our technological advances in such areas as collective and artificial intelligence, you may have new ways to collect and analyze data. If so, explicate the fallacies of the most closely aligned traditions for your research question and explain how a recombination of varied methods or the invention of new methods address these fallacies. You may become the forebearer of a new qualitative research tradition.

When refining an overarching research question, I think it is especially helpful to rotate through varied research traditions. What would your research question be if it were, among others, an ethnography, phenomenology, case study, narrative inquiry, biography, grounded theory study, or content analysis study? I return to the sample:

> *Given a postpositivist paradigm, what is the nature of literacy in a technology-rich fourth-grade classroom from a sociocultural perspective using ethnographic research methods?*

Consider how the study would change if I inserted different research traditions.

> *What is the nature of literacy… using…*
>
> *ethnographic research methods?*
>
> *phenomenological research methods?*
>
> *case study research methods?*
>
> *narrative inquiry research methods?*
>
> *biographical research methods?*
>
> *grounded theory methods?*
>
> *content analysis research methods?*

In Table 3.1, I provide a flavor for how tradition substitutions might impact the Anatomy. Alterations to the sample research question could be varied but I provide samples as fodder for your consideration.

If I return to the sample question and reposition it as a phenomenology, it might be formulated as follows:

> *Given a postpositivist paradigm, what is the ~~nature of literacy~~ [lived experience of reading and writing] among fourth-graders in a technology-rich classroom from a sociocultural perspective using ~~ethnographic~~ [phenomenological] research methods?*

When phenomenology is substituted for ethnography, the focus of the study shifts from understanding the cultural norms of a technology-rich fourth-grade classroom to focusing on individuals who have had the lived experience of reading and writing with technology in the designated fourth-grade classroom. My primary data set shifts from observation notes to in-depth interviews (e.g., Seidman, 2019). My report shifts from describing 3–5 characteristics or themes regarding the nature of literacy to 3–5 characteristics or themes regarding a lived experience. One of the affordances of phenomenology is that researchers can design studies that reside outside of time and space. Ethnography purposely examines a topic in a certain time and place. While phenomenology can be designed to target a phenomenon that occurred at a specific time and place

TABLE 3.1 ■ Qualitative Research Traditions: Explore Substitutions

Qualitative Research Tradition	Focus of Tradition	Sample Research Questions
Ethnography (sample question)	Study of specified topic within a particular culture	What is the nature of literacy in a technology-rich fourth-grade classroom...
Phenomenology	Study of specified lived experience—commonly regardless of context	What is the lived experience of reading and writing with digital technologies...
Case Study	Study of a bounded system regarding specified topic	What is the nature of literacy in Ms. Smith's technology-rich fourth-grade classroom between January and February...
Narrative Inquiry	Study of narratives as they relate to specified topic	What are the stories of fourth graders who use 1:1 information and communication technologies in their classroom...
Biography	Study of someone's life—which is the topic	What is Ms. Smith's life story (teacher of the fourth-grade classroom), progenitor of digital information, and communication literacies...
Grounded Theory	Generate theories that explain origins and predict future of specified topic	Where did literacy come from and where is it going...
Content Analysis	Examine artifacts to make sense of topic	What is the nature of literacy in a technology-rich fourth-grade classroom's online discussion board...

(e.g., what was the lived experience of surviving COVID-19 among those who worked in NYC emergency rooms in 2020), it can also transcend time and place (e.g., what is the lived experience of being a graduate student).

As a Case Study, the sample question will specify a bounded system. The binding might be a certain time, specific place, among a particular group, or any combination. A bounded system can be very large (e.g., within a country, across a decade) or very small (e.g., among a group of children in a specific classroom during a specific activity). The size of the bounded system will depend on the related literature. Does the study need to be large or small or somewhere in between to contribute to current concepts?

As a case study, the sample question might become:

> *Given a postpositivist paradigm, what is the nature of literacy in ~~a~~ [Ms. Smith's] technology-rich fourth-grade classroom from a sociocultural perspective using ~~ethnographic~~ [case study] research methods?*

The revised question might benefit from a specific timeframe. As currently stated, the bounded system appears to include an entire school year. There is nothing inherently right or wrong about this large timeframe. Again, the terms you use to bind your system will likely be determined by what will push your field forward. Case study research methods invoke a broad array of data collection and analysis methods. You might collect observation notes, video/audio recordings, interview data, and artifacts as well as any quantitative data that help you understand the case.

As implied by its name, narrative inquiry is focused on telling the participants' stories as they relate to a shared experience. The sample question might therefore be revised to ask:

> *Given a postpositivist paradigm, what ~~is the nature of literacy in a technology-rich fourth-grade classroom~~ [are the stories of fourth graders who use 1:1 information and communication technologies in their classroom] from a sociocultural perspective using ~~ethnographic~~ [narrative inquiry] research methods?*

A narrative report will be very different from ethnographic or phenomenological reports which typically coalesce findings around 3–5 emergent characteristics or themes. In other words, when you write ethnographic and phenomenological research reports, the headings will commonly feature characteristics or themes. When you write a narrative research report, the headings may feature participants.

For me, another distinction of a narrative inquiry is the paradigmatic view of the researcher. While a postpositivist understands that the researcher and participants cannot be isolated, the postpositivist deals with this inevitable coalescence by purposely documenting and analyzing his role from initial contact, to field entry, to established perceptions of participants of the researcher's role. The postpositivist makes decisions about where he resides on a continuum between the participant and observer, systematically documents when and how his role shifts along this continuum, and reports, to the best of his ability, his own obtrusiveness in the setting. Those who conduct narrative inquiry simply acknowledge that their presence is part of the study. The researcher is viewed as a participant and therefore his story is included in data collection, data analyses, and research reports. Given these paradigmatic implications, the research question might be restated as:

> *Given a ~~postpositivist~~ [constructivist, critical] paradigm, what ~~is the nature of literacy in a technology-rich fourth-grade classroom~~ [are the stories of fourth graders who use 1:1 information and communication technologies in their classroom] from a sociocultural perspective using ~~ethnographic~~ [narrative inquiry] research methods?*

In the sample question, I deleted postpositivist and inserted constructivist and critical paradigms. It is important to avoid the notion that all researchers within a particular paradigm use a certain set of research traditions. Rather, researchers with different paradigms may use the same research traditions but for varied ontological and epistemological reasons (see Appendix B). Narrative inquiry is a good fit for those who believe reality exists within the story.

Before I proceed to the next tradition, I should point out that if the question is posed by a constructivist, then the researcher will employ corresponding theoretical perspectives such as social learning theories or socio-cognition, among others. If posed by a critical theorist, then the researcher may find critical race theory, feminism, queer theory, posthumanism, and postcolonialism, among an array of options, to provide useful theoretical groundings. In other words, paradigmatic shifts may invoke theoretical shifts. (See Section: *Substitute the Theoretical Perspective(s).*)

So far, I have discussed implications for changing the sample question from an ethnography to a phenomenology, case study, or narrative inquiry. If my sample question were a biography, I might ask:

> *Given a postpositivist paradigm, what is ~~the nature of literacy in a technology-rich fourth-grade classroom~~ [Ms. Smith's life story (teacher of*

> *the fourth-grade classroom), progenitor of digital information and communication literacies] from a sociocultural perspective using ~~ethnographic~~ [biographical] research methods?*

The focus of this study would shift from understanding the nature of literacy in a particular classroom during specified months to understanding the life story of a person—in this case, the teacher of the fourth-grade classroom, Ms. Smith. A biography might be conducted by postpositivists, constructivists, critical theorists, and poststructuralists. The role of the researcher would be viewed differently and reported accordingly. The theoretical perspective(s) would likely change and align with the paradigm. But the essence of the report would be to tell the life story, birth to death (or current point in life), of one person. If the person is living, then data collection might focus on interviews with the person being studied as well as those associated with her. If the person is deceased, then data collection might focus on those who remain living, first-hand accounts, and first-hand artifacts (e.g., letters, speeches, etc.). Keep in mind, all researchers make paradigmatic and theoretical assumptions. While the genre of biography doesn't typically explicate these assumptions, if you plan to conduct a biography, I recommend that you recognize your own assumptions. This will help you justify why your biography has the potential to provide new insights and why your committee, funding agency, or publisher should support your work.

Let's see what happens if I formulate my question as a grounded theory study. First, I must recognize that grounded theory is another term that is conflated. Some refer to grounded theory as findings that are derived from (grounded in) the data (see Strauss & Corbin, 1990). Others refer to grounded theory as a research tradition that seeks to theorize the origins of a topic so as to predict the future of that topic (see Birks & Mills, 2015; Charmaz, 2006). For my purposes, I am referring to grounded theory as a research tradition. If I were to ask the sample question as a grounded theory study (tradition), it might be phrased accordingly:

> *Given a postpositivist paradigm, ~~what is the nature of~~ [what theories explain the origins of] literacy ~~in a technology-rich fourth-grade classroom from a sociocultural perspective~~ [and how do these theories help predict the future of literacy] using ~~ethnographic~~ [grounded theory] research methods?*

I find this to be an intriguing question—but not the essence of what I want to learn in this particular study. Similar to other substituted traditions, I would need to specify what I mean by literacy. I might focus on the origins of written expression. In which case, the related literature would be entirely different than the literature used to conduct the specified ethnography which would tap into related literature about the basic characteristics that define literacy (nature of literacy). For a grounded theory study, I would draw from the history of written expression and possibly the purpose of communication.

The goal of a grounded theory study is to generate a theory of origins that might predict continuation or conclusion of the topic being studied. For me, a perfect example of a grounded theory study is Darwin's (1859) *On the Origins of Species*. He posited that species came to be as they are through a grounded theory he called evolution. He then used this grounded theory to predict the continuation and/or final demise of species. While Darwin's theory of evolution was derived from (grounded in) data, the foci of the study was to generate a theory of existence that could be used to make predictions for future existence. I think it is safe to say that all robust, trustworthy qualitative findings are derived from (grounded in) the data. However, grounded theory as a research tradition seeks to generate a coherent theory that explains how a topic emerged and predict where it might go. The research report, therefore, will differ from ethnographies, phenomenologies, and cases (e.g., 3–5 characteristics or themes) as well as narrative inquiries or biographies (e.g., stories). Grounded theory reports focus on explaining the emergence of the theory and the predictive implications of the theory.

My final tradition is content analysis. As stated, content analysis can refer to a method and a tradition. When studies collect multiple types of data (e.g., observation, interview, artifacts), they might use content analysis to make sense of the artifact data. Therefore, content analysis is one type of data analysis (method) used within the broader study. However, some studies consist of collecting and analyzing only artifacts. In this case, content analysis might be employed as a research tradition. The sample research question might be transformed as follows:

> *Given a postpositivist paradigm, what is the nature of literacy in a technology-rich fourth-grade classroom ['s online discussion board] from a sociocultural perspective using ~~ethnographic~~ [content analysis] research methods?*

Framed as a content analysis study, using constant comparison (Glaser, 1965), I would analyze the online discussion board. Content analysis studies lend themselves to both open and a priori coding. **Open coding** begins with theoretical perspective(s) and codes from the specified lens(es). Codes emerge and are refined through constant comparison. **A priori coding** begins with constructs and codes for those constructs. For example, to make sense of how classroom web sites were being used to support literacy, I coded classroom web site features using predetermined instructional approaches (Baker, 2007). In another study, a doctoral student wanted to identify the recommendations that literacy researchers might provide to principals and policymakers. She therefore coded the transcripts of a popular journal-based podcast that featured interviews with literacy researchers who were consistently asked, based on their study, what would they tell principals and policymakers. In both cases, the data were artifact only. If open coding is used, the content analysis report will describe 3–5 characteristics or themes that emerged while coding. If a priori coding is used, the report will describe how the findings coalesced around constructs of a predetermined framework and may posit a revision to the framework.

Positioning your work within several research traditions can help you refine your question. Each tradition invokes corresponding data collection and analysis methods. Each tradition shifts the focus of the study. Each tradition represents divergent research report genres. When you recapitulate your topic according to varied traditions, you can critique the substance, methods, potential findings, and research report genre of your study. You can consider which tradition helps you hone your question. Or you can consider the shortcomings of current traditions and formulate your own strategies that help you answer your research question. I recommend that you return to this substitution often.

Substitute the Setting

Another substitution that can facilitate honing the design of your qualitative study is the setting. The sample research question specified that the study would be conducted in a technology-rich fourth-grade classroom. Given the topic, nature of literacy, the setting completely changes the focus of the study. Consider how the study would change if I inserted different settings.

What is the nature of literacy in a ...

fourth-grade technology-rich classroom?

fourth-grade print-based classroom?

technology-rich home with children ages 6–12 years?

online social media platform (e.g., Facebook, Instagram)?

retirement center?

Making substitutions to the setting may unearth possibilities you had not considered. Brainstorm. Be outrageous. What is the nature of literacy on Mars? Think outside of the box. Go back through related literature and make a list of the settings. Maybe the contribution of your study is that it is conducted in a new setting.

Substitute the Theoretical Perspective(s)

A final substitution you might play with is your theoretical perspective(s). If you are unsure of your perspective(s), I pose a few strategies to help you unearth your theoretical perspective(s) and articulate your intuition. First, and possibly most obvious, generate a list of theoretical perspectives used in your field. Go to the top journals in your field that publish qualitative research and make a list of the theories that researchers use to define their terms, determine what qualifies as data (and what does not qualify), and inform the rationale for their study.

Second, you can identify theoretical perspectives taken by other fields. Maybe you can shed new light on your field by illuminating it with perspectives forged in other fields but are nascent in your own field. If you are an engineer, what perspectives have been used by economists? medical researchers? geographers? psychologists? Might the theoretical assumptions used in other fields be coopted and used to inform your field? I purport that examining a topic from a new lens has the potential to extend the current knowledge base of a field.

Third, it might be helpful to take a gestalt view of the history of your field. For example, literacy has been examined using a wide range of theories derived from such fields as behavioral psychology, neurology, linguistics, psycholinguistics, semiotics, cognitive psychology, sociology, and feminist studies. Theories derived from these fields have produced interesting theoretical mash-ups. For example, insights from sociology and cognitive psychology have produced useful theories of sociocognition. Insights from sociology and linguistics have provided insights derived from sociolinguistics. Maybe your field has historically invoked an economic or systems view. It might be helpful to identify the perspectives taken by those whose work you hope to extend or refute.

For example, historically, behavioral psychology launched modern research in my field, literacy, by focusing on the reading process. Similar to

Pavlov's dogs, reading was examined in terms of stimulus response. Based on stimulus-response theories, it was argued that you can teach a child to read by conditioning her responses to letters in the alphabet. When a child sees the letters C A T, an initial conditioned response may be to name the letters. The next conditioned response may be to make a match between the letters and the sounds they make (e.g., /k/, /æ/, /t/). Finally, you can condition the learner to blend these sounds to make an accurate match between C A T (the letters) and *cat* (the oral word). If I substitute stimulus-response theory into my sample question, it would be:

> *Given a postpositivist paradigm, what is the nature of literacy in a technology-rich fourth-grade classroom from a ~~sociocultural~~ [stimulus-response] perspective using ethnographic research methods?*

Hopefully, you are familiar enough with stimulus-response theory to see several Anatomy mismatches. Can you see the mismatches with the paradigm? topic? setting? and tradition? Paradigmatically, stimulus-response theory is rooted in objective reality. There is a right and wrong answer: C is the letter C; not the letters ABDE or F. In this case, the letter C makes a specific sound, /k/. While sounds will vary by language and dialect, there are corresponding right and wrong sounds. The knower has no impact on the reality that a C is a C and CAT spells the oral word, *cat*. Stimulus-response theory aligns well with positivism. So, if I were to view reading from a stimulus-response perspective, I would likely need to reconsider my paradigm. My revised question would be:

> *Given a ~~postpositivist~~ [positivist] paradigm, what is the nature of literacy in a technology-rich fourth-grade classroom from a ~~sociocultural~~ [stimulus-response] perspective using ethnographic research methods?*

The topic, nature of literacy, is misaligned with stimulus-response. So the topic would need to change. Maybe research from a stimulus-response perspective would focus on accuracy rates. In which case, the question would become:

> *Given a ~~postpositivist~~ [positivist] paradigm, what is the ~~nature of literacy~~ [accuracy rate] in a technology-rich fourth-grade classroom from a ~~sociocultural~~ [stimulus-response] perspective using ethnographic research methods?*

I would then need to specify accuracy rates of what and provide a viable reason (e.g., accuracy rate for saying/cat/when exposed to the letters CAT).

Ethnography as well as a technology-rich classroom are not particularly useful when conducting a study focused on accuracy rates for CAT. Thus, because of my perspective, stimulus-response, I need to change my paradigm, topic, setting, and tradition.

If I return to the history of literacy research, the field was revolutionized by cognitive psychology and schema theory (Bransford & Johnson, 1972; Rumelhart, 1980) which argues that humans structure knowledge into related constructs called schema. When a schema perspective was used to understand the reading process, the focus shifted from phonics (e.g., *cat* is the oral word for CAT) to comprehension. From a schema-theory perspective, the ability to make a match between the letters CAT and the sounds /k//æ//t/ and the oral word, *cat*, was vapid unless the reader made a connection to the furry pet with a long twitching tail that purrs. Accuracy rates were superfluous without comprehension. If schema-theory were substituted in the sample question, it would be:

> *Given a postpositivist paradigm, what is the nature of literacy in a technology-rich fourth-grade classroom from a ~~sociocultural~~ [schema-theory] perspective using ethnographic research methods?*

Varied cognitive research methods were used to understand reading comprehension as a schema-based activity. One of my favorite examples was a study conducted by Bransford and Johnson (1972). They composed an ambiguous paragraph that described the process of washing clothes—without ever mentioning detergent, machine, or clothes. The adult subjects were asked to read the paragraph and retell it as accurately as possible. Most were unable to recall the information and exhibited low comprehension scores. However, when they were told the paragraph was about washing clothes, they were able to readily retell the story with a full complement of supporting details. Bransford and Johnson describe their study as experimental. They used control groups, pre- and posttests, mean comprehension ratings, and *p* scores. If I substitute schema-theory into the sample question, based on Bransford and Johnson's research methods, this study would no longer be a qualitative study. The question would be rooted in positivism and best addressed with experimental research methods.

A fourth strategy for unearthing your assumptions (theoretical lens) is to define your **data collection unit (DCU)**. What do/don't you deem to be data for your study? When I conducted my dissertation, I needed to determine when literacy occurred in the technology-rich classroom. Should I collect data whenever students encountered alphabetic text? Should I ignore multimodal (e.g., video, audio files, animations, dataviz) texts? Using a sociocultural lens, which embraces multimodal texts, I was able to ascertain that nonalphabetic texts would be included in my DCU.

Fifth, you can generate a list of potential findings to your research question. Returning to the sample question, one of the findings was that literacy in this technology-rich classroom was public. Students constantly read one another's screens. They could see classmates' screens from where they sat. During informal interviews, students readily told me what each of their neighbors were writing about. In addition, the teacher encouraged students to solicit feedback from classmates. Before a composition was turned in, they invited classmates to their screens to read and discuss the composition. They conducted inquiry projects that culminated in presentations of their findings. The students read and wrote for and with an audience. A characteristic of literacy in this classroom was that reading and writing were public. While you will pontificate on *possible* findings, I already know that a finding from the sample question was the literacy in this particular classroom was public. Given actual or hypothetical findings, you can consider the assumptions made to garner this finding. For example, behavioral theories would help me consider the stimulus-response events in this classroom. Cognitive theories would help me focus on the thought processes, decisions, made by students as they read and wrote. Sociocultural theories helped me consider the cultural norms of the classroom (e.g., students read one another's screens from their seats, teacher encouraged students to solicit feedback). Your lens helps you to make sense of your data. If you are unaware of your lens, start making sense of data and consider the assumptions you are making. Then, identify the theories that inform your assumptions.

A final strategy you might use to identify your lens is to explain the implications of your potential findings. This exercise requires you to take a stance that inherently invokes perspective. For example, if literacy is public, if students in this technology-rich classroom consistently read one another's screens and received solicited as well as unsolicited feedback, then the notion of assessing an individual student's growth (e.g., give grades) may be bogus. This implication is rooted in sociocultural theory which views the role of cultural norms. In this case, the consistent interactions between author and audience make it difficult to claim that the author and audience are distinct (see Baker, Rozendal, & Whitenack, 2000). Given a sociocultural perspective, this begs the question: If author and audience are indistinct, can grades be assigned to the author? Give it a try! What are the implications of your potential findings? What stance(s) do you take in order to make such claims? Answers may reveal your assumptions/lens(es).

When you identify your perspective(s) before you conduct your study, you are empowered to explain how your work compares with those who take the same perspective but different interrogatives, topics, settings, and paradigm as well as those who take different perspectives but similar interrogatives, topics, settings, and paradigm. Your perspective(s) provide footholds for discussing the implications and significance of your findings. If you struggle to interpret your findings or discuss the significance of your findings, you likely need to clarify your theoretical perspective(s).

I have mentioned some terms that are commonly conflated. For example, grounded theory can refer to findings being derived from (grounded in) the data as well as a research tradition. Language evolves. Users take up the same words when they refer to dissimilar concepts. The same is true of some theoretical perspectives and paradigms. For example, some use constructivism, critical, and poststructuralism to refer to theoretical perspectives. I prefer to disaggregate these terms. I prefer to avoid using paradigmatic and theoretical terms interchangeably. I contend that disaggregation fosters clarity and provides fodder for advancing both paradigmatic axioms and theoretical tenets. For example, you can focus on learning as a topic and/or employ social learning theories and sociocognitive perspectives without being a constructivist. Similarly, you can be passionate about injustices, racism, and issues related to dis/empowerment without being paradigmatically critical. When you disaggregate the terms used for paradigms from perspectives, you can formulate research that is rooted in paradigmatic truth while pursuing topics and employing theories you are passionate about.

Reformulate your study according to varied and divergent perspectives. Go out on a limb. Go radical. Then identify which theoretical perspective(s) you want to use for the purposes of your current study. Note: It is possible to take multiple perspectives within one study. It is also possible, given a rich data set, to conduct several different analyses based on different perspectives. The power of substituting perspectives cannot be underscored enough.

WORK THE MARBLE: IMPLICATIONS OF SUBSTITUTIONS

To facilitate substitutions, I recommend that you write the six parts of the Anatomy, and varied substitutions, on index cards or in the cells of a spreadsheet/table (see Table 3.2) or use Worksheet 3.1. These index cards, spreadsheet/table, or Worksheet 3.1 become the proverbial marble that you

TABLE 3.2 ■ Working the Marble: Mix and Match the Anatomy

Paradigm	Interrogative	Substance (Topic)	Setting	Theoretical Perspective	Tradition
Positivist **Postpositivist** Constructivist Critical Poststructuralist	What	Nature of Literacy	Technology-rich fourth-grade classroom	Sociocultural	Ethnography
Postpositivist	Who **What** Where When Why How	Nature of Literacy	Technology-rich fourth-grade classroom	Sociocultural	Ethnography
		Nature of Literacy Impact on paragraph organization Make meaning of and with digital texts Empowered to communicate Binaries			
Postpositivist	What	Nature of Literacy	**Technology-rich fourth-grade classroom**	Sociocultural	Ethnography

(Continued)

TABLE 3.2 ■ Working the Marble: Mix and Match the Anatomy (Continued)

			Print-based fourth-grade classroom Online social media platform (e.g., Facebook, Instagram) Retirement center		
Postpositivist	What	Nature of Literacy	Technology-rich fourth-grade classroom	Behavioral Neurological Linguistic Psycholinguistic Semiotic Cognitive Sociological Sociocognitive **Sociocultural** Feminist Queer Posthumanistic	Ethnography
Postpositivist	What	Nature of Literacy	Technology-rich fourth-grade classroom	Sociocultural	**Ethnography** Phenomenology Narrative Inquiry Case Study Content Analysis
Resultant Research Question:					
Postpositivist	What	Nature of Literacy	Technology-rich fourth-grade classroom	Sociocultural	Ethnography

chisel, chip, sand, and play with until you shape a satisfactory overarching question for your study. Shuffle the substitutions in and out of your question.

You will see that in Table 3.2, I do not highlight the substitution of the topic (substance) for the study. This will change according to the substitutions made to the other parts of the Anatomy. In other words, systematically making substitutions with each part of the Anatomy will give you fodder to refine your substance (topic). You can then consider which substitutions help you identify the essence of your study—your topic. Make substitutions. Reformulate your research question. Consider: Is that what I want to study? Revise the substance (topic). Repeat. Repeat. Repeat.

Align the Parts of the Anatomy

As you make substitutions, confirm that the parts of the Anatomy remain aligned. When you change one part of the Anatomy, there are implications for other parts. As described throughout this chapter, when you change the interrogative, tradition, setting, and perspective(s), the topic will shift. Be sure to align the topic accordingly. In Chapter 2, I claimed that asking research questions can help you examine your paradigmatic assumptions. This is a good time to consider the ramifications of invoking varied paradigms (see Table 2.1). Does your paradigm align with your interrogative, perspective(s), and tradition? You want to avoid a disjointed Anatomy that resembles Frankenstein or a Zombie. For example, the following substitutions are misaligned. Can you see why?

> *Given a ~~postpositivist~~ [critical] paradigm, what is the nature of literacy ~~in a technology-rich fourth-grade classroom~~ [in a classroom social media platform] from a ~~sociocultural~~ [cognitive] perspective using ~~ethnographic~~ [phenomenological] research methods?*

First, a critical paradigm views reality in terms of power. While a critical researcher may be interested in understanding literacy as it occurs on a social media platform, the theoretical lens would be focused on who is empowered and disempowered—not on cognitive thought processes. In addition, critical views of reality can be mismatched with phenomenology because the focus of phenomenology is to understand the participants' lived experience. The primary data set is in-depth interviews which, when used during a phenomenology, invoke strict guidelines to minimize, as much as is possible, asking questions that indicate the response the interviewer is hoping to hear (see Seidman, 2019). When I have worked with critical researchers, systematic analyses of the questions they asked revealed consistent tendencies to ask the participants if they were empowered or disempowered (see Chapter 4: *Susan, Feeding Newborns*). Unless the participants generate this information, researchers using established procedures for phenomenology cannot ask such questions—unless of course the lived experience being studied is dis/empowerment. Thus, this question has a mismatch between paradigm, theoretical perspective, and research tradition.

Reconsider Potential Answers

While you make the aforementioned substitutions to the interrogative, tradition, setting perspective, paradigm, and align the parts (which includes tweaking the topic), reconsider hypothetical answers to your reformulated question. This may feel counterintuitive. After all, you have not conducted the study—so how can you generate potential answers? If you knew the answers, you wouldn't be conducting the study. What I am suggesting is that you generate *potential* answers. I find this strategy to be invaluable when deciding whether my question cuts to the core of what I strive to learn. I return to the sample question:

> *Given a postpositivist paradigm, what is the nature of literacy in a technology-rich fourth-grade classroom from a sociocultural perspective using ethnographic research methods?*

What are the potential answers to this question? The interrogative, topic, setting, perspective, tradition, and paradigm indicate that this study will generate characteristics of the nature of literacy. Because this sample question is derived from an actual study, I can tell you that the findings indicated that the nature of literacy in this technology-rich classroom was semiotic, public, transitory, and product/ion oriented (Baker, 2001, 2020; Baker et al., 2015). If you are disappointed that the findings from your study will generate 3–5 characteristics or themes, then avoid formulating your question accordingly. If you want to tell participants' stories, consider reformulating your work as a narrative inquiry or biography. If you want to generate a theory to explain how something came to be as it is and use the corresponding theory to predict where it is going, consider asking a grounded theory question.

I already gave examples of what might happen when you change the interrogative. In the sample, when I changed *What* to *How*, then potential answers shifted the focus of the study from characteristics of literacy to the steps that participants took to use technology to read and write. When I changed *What* to *Who*, then potential answers might generate a list of the participants. In the example of changing the setting from a technology-rich fourth-grade classroom to a print-based fourth-grade classroom, the answers might involve the nature of literacy as meaning based, skills based, student centered, and curriculum centered. I have to ask myself, "Are these the sorts of findings I want to generate? Will this question reveal truth and reality about my passion?"

This is a good time to revisit your paradigm. You may be fully cognizant of your paradigm. In which case, there is no need to substitute paradigms and consider potential answers to your question. Conversely, you may be striving to understand your paradigm. In this case, reformulating your research question according to varied paradigms can help you do some soul-searching. For example, reformulating my sample question based on critical paradigmatic tenets, I might align my theoretical perspective to sociolinguistics, and generate the following question:

> *Given a critical paradigm, what is the nature of ~~literacy~~ [empowerment during reading and writing activities that occur] in a fourth-grade classroom from a sociolinguistic perspective using ethnographic research methods?*

This question may generate 3–5 characteristics or themes of the nature of empowerment that expose who is empowered and disempowered during literacy practices in this classroom. Are these the sort of findings you want to discover? If so, great! You may have formulated your research question. If the findings do not expose the kinds of findings you want to unearth, then continue varied substitutions and consider potential findings.

Reconsider Potential Report Genre

In this section, I return to the notion of genre. While substituting traditions, I mentioned implications for corresponding reports. In Table 3.3, I bring together this information so you can reconsider your question in terms of genre. Noting the genres that are inherent to each research tradition may facilitate your ability to brainstorm possible findings and reformulate your research question. In other words, each tradition has a corresponding report genre. For example, an ethnographic report might describe 3–5 characteristics or themes of the culture where the study was conducted. A phenomenology might describe 3–5 characteristics or themes

TABLE 3.3 ■ Research Traditions: Possible Report Genres

Qualitative Research Tradition	Focus of Tradition	Report Genre Options
Ethnography (sample question)	Study of culture regarding specified topic	3–5 Characteristics/ Themes of the topic within specific culture
Phenomenology	Study of specified lived experience—regardless of context	3–5 Characteristics/ Themes of the lived experience
Case Study	Study of a bounded system regarding specified topic	3–5 Characteristics/ Themes of the case
Narrative Inquiry	Study of narratives as they relate to specified topic	The stories of several people involved in the same/similar event
Biography	Study of someone's life—which is the topic	The life story of one person
Grounded Theory	Generate theories that explain origins and evolution of specified topic	Theory, grounded in data, that explains where findings came from to assert where the topic might be going (e.g., evolution explains the origins of the species)

of the lived experience of a phenomenon. A narrative inquiry will tell stories of several participants engaged in similar activities while a biography will trace the life of a particular person. Consider whether you want to describe 3–5 characteristics or themes of a culture or a lived experience, tell stories of several participants as they relate to the topic, or the life story of one person. I defer to the books that have been written about sundry qualitative research traditions as well as your own perusal of research reports to grasp the varied and rich array of qualitative research report genres (see Chapter 3: *Suggested Readings*). I find that considering the genre of the final report can facilitate chiseling away at your idea in pursuit of a finely crafted qualitative research question.

CHAPTER SUMMARY

In Chapter 3, I described three metacognitive strategies that occur simultaneously and can be used to refine your research question. These strategies include making substitutions to the six parts of the Anatomy, considering hypothetical answers, and rephrasing the question to suit varied genres. In the end, the anatomical parts of your research question must align. Generating possible answers to your question may help you determine whether your emerging question reveals the core of your passions. Finally, consideration of your report genre can help you finalize your question.

In Chapter 4, I contextualize these strategies by telling composite stories of Bert, a conservationist, and Susan, a nurse. They came to me with topics they wanted to explore. Using the Anatomy and metacognitive strategies detailed in Chapters 1–3, we drafted, brainstormed, revised, and brainstormed some more until their passions and intuitions were transformed into research questions imbued with the components of a full-fledged proposal.

SUGGESTED ACTIVITIES AND DISCUSSIONS

1. Interrogatives: Using a simple topic, discuss the implications of each interrogative. For example, what are the answers to the following questions: Who, what, where, when, why, and how did you go to a recent movie? Alter the syntax as needed. For example, Who did I go to a recent movie can be discussed as, With whom did I go to a recent movie? Discuss how the interrogative shifts the focus of the question. Then apply the varied implications of interrogatives to your emerging research question.

2. Guess My Tradition: Write research traditions on slips of paper. Each person picks a slip. Without revealing what you picked, formulate a corresponding research question. Describe what data you plan to collect and why. Describe what data analyses you plan to conduct and why. Describe the format of your final report. Let others ask you about your study until they can identify your research tradition. Research questions can be focused on your research interests, transpositions of a research question from a familiar research report (as done with the sample question used through this book), or perfunctory topics (e.g., dinner, exercise, vacation, entertainment). As a group, you might select a topic before you pick slips of paper and see if everyone can formulate questions focused on the same topic using varied traditions. Use the traditions discussed in this chapter or others that may be pertinent to your research (e.g., ethnomethodology, autoethnography, self-study, Discourse Analysis, action research, formative experiments, design-based experiments, hermeneutics, etc.).

3. Settings: Go through related literature and make a list of the settings. Brainstorm other settings for your study. Discuss whether you want to conduct your study in a setting that is similar or distinct from previous studies.

4a. Role of Perspective, The State Fair: To grapple with the role of perspective, create slips of paper with any/all of the following roles:

- 6-year-old child
- Teenager
- Parent
- Livestock, bakery, vegetable entrant of your choice (e.g., farmer, 4H Club Member)
- Livestock judge
- Bakery goods judge
- Vegetable judge
- Police officer
- Ticket salesperson
- Game booth operator
- Ferris wheel operator
- Soloist for rock and roll band booked to perform
- Grounds keeper
- News reporter of your choice (e.g., TV, newspaper, online media outlets)

Put the slips of paper in a jar and each person picks one slip from the jar. Without disclosing your role, take turns describing your expectations, interests, and concerns while attending the State Fair. See if you can guess one another's role (perspective) at the State Fair. Discuss how perspective influences your view of the situation. Discuss the implications of perspective while collecting and analyzing qualitative data.

4b. Role of Perspective, Your Discipline: You may prefer to complete Suggested Activity 4a and/or select a setting that is applicable to you. Similar to the State Fair in 4a, create a list of roles for your setting. If your setting is a hospital, you might list doctors, nurses, technicians, corporate officers, trustees, patients, patient families, and others. If your setting is a place of business, maybe a coffee shop, you might list franchise owner, shift manager, employee, contracted advertising manager/employee, contracted distribution manager/ employee, adult customer, child customer, and others.

Similar to Activity 4a, without disclosure, distribute the roles. Take turns describing your expectations, interests, and concerns as per your role. Discuss how role influences your view of the situation. Discuss how roles translate to perspective and the implications of perspective while conducting qualitative research.

5. Unearth Your Perspective, The Nature of Gardens: To explore how perspective informs delineation of your DCU, potential findings as well as implications, go online and find 3–5 images of gardens. If you are completing this activity with a group, post the images to a shared space (e.g., GoogleDocs). To explore how perspective informs the following:
   a. DCU: Consider/discuss why you chose some images but not others. It is possible that answers will reveal your assumptions (theories) about gardens.
   b. Data analysis: List the characteristics of Image 1 (e.g., includes flowers, trees, bushes). Next, list the characteristics of Image 2 (e.g., is on a rooftop, includes a swimming pool). Then, merge the characteristics of Images 1 and 2. You may need to extrapolate into broader categories. Flowers, trees, and bushes may become Living Plants, while rooftop may become Location and swimming pool may become Nonliving Structures. Now, add Image 3. Refine your categories. Continue this process for 5–10 images. If any image is discarded, justify your decision. Merge the categories into 3–5 characteristics or themes. If any category is discarded, justify your decision. Throughout this process, consider the role of perspective in generating characteristics, categories, and/or themes.
   c. Interpretation of findings: Based on the 3–5 characteristics that emerged, take on varied roles (e.g., botanist, painter, landscape architect, farmer, rabbit, carrot) and make recommendations about gardens. Consider how perspective (e.g., role) informs your recommendations. Extrapolate how theoretical perspective informs insights you glean from findings when you conduct your own study.
6. Brainstorm theoretical perspectives you might take. Use the five strategies described in Chapter 3: *Substitute the Theoretical Perspectives:*
   a. Go through related literature and make a list of the theoretical perspectives.
   b. Consider theoretical perspectives taken in other fields that might enlighten your field.
   c. Consider the historical roots of your field as well as possible mash-ups (e.g., sociology and linguistics provided theories of sociolinguistics).
   d. Define your DCU. When you look at a transcript, how do you know what to code? What "counts" as data? The assumptions you make to define your DCU are rooted in your theoretical perspective.
   e. Generate a list of potential findings and consider the assumptions you make to generate these findings. These assumptions are rooted in your theoretical perspective.

7. Make several copies of Worksheet 3.1. Circle varied combinations of the Anatomy. Consider and discuss whether combinations are aligned. Purposely create some ghastly combinations so you can practice identifying aligned and misaligned components of the Anatomy.
8. Identify combinations from Worksheet 3.1 that are aligned. To refine your options, consider the potential answers. Do you care about what the answers might be? If vapid, revise or select other options.
9. To further refine your research question, consider the report genre (see Table 3.3). Do you want to generate a report with 3–5 characteristics/themes? stories of those involved in a common experience? a biography? a theory that explains origins and might predict the future? Revise the combinations you selected on Worksheet 3.1 to align with the report genre you hope to produce.
10. Revisit your paradigmatic assumptions (see Table 2.1). According to your paradigm, does your question pursue reality? How does your question need to be revised to grapple with reality?

SUGGESTED READINGS

Biography

Denzin, N. (1989). *Interpretive biography*. Thousand Oaks, CA: SAGE.

Goodwin, J. (2012). *SAGE biographical research*, Vol. 1–4. Thousand Oaks, CA: SAGE.

Case Study

Stake, R. E. (1995). *The art of case study research*. Thousand Oaks, CA: SAGE.

Yin, R. K. (2017). *Case study research and applications: Design and methods*. Thousand Oaks, CA: SAGE.

Content Analysis Study

Krippendorff, K. (2004). *Content analysis: An introduction to its methodology* (2nd ed.). Thousand Oaks, CA: SAGE.

Schreier, M. (2012). *Qualitative content analysis in practice*. Thousand Oaks, CA: SAGE.

Ethnography

Atkinson, P. (2001). *Handbook of ethnography*. London: SAGE.

Hammersley, M., & Atkinson, P. (2019). *Ethnography: Principles in practice* (4th ed.). New York, NY: Routledge.

Heath, S. B., & Street, B. V. (2008). *On ethnography: Approaches to language and literacy research*. New York, NY: Teachers College Press.

Grounded Theory

Birks, M., & Mills, J. (2015). *Grounded theory: A practical guide* (2nd ed.). London: SAGE.

Charmaz, K. (2006). *Constructing grounded theory: A practical guide through qualitative analysis.* Thousand Oaks, CA: SAGE.

Strauss, A., & Corbin, J. (1990). *Basics of qualitative research: Grounded theory procedures and techniques.* Thousand Oaks, CA: SAGE.

Narrative Inquiry

Clandinin, J. (Ed.) (2007). *Handbook of narrative inquiry: Mapping a methodology.* Thousand Oaks, CA: SAGE.

Clandinin, D. J. & Connelly, F. M. (2000). *Narrative inquiry: Experience and story in qualitative research.* San Francisco, CA: Jossey-Bass Publishers.

Phenomenology

Moustakas, C. E. (1994). *Phenomenological research methods*. Thousand Oaks, CA: SAGE.

Seidman, I. (2019). *Interviewing as qualitative research: A guide for researchers in education and social sciences* (5th ed.). New York, NY: Teachers College Press.

Vagle, M. D. (2018). *Crafting phenomenological research* (2nd ed.). New York, NY: Routledge.

van Manen, M. (2016). *Phenomenology of practice*. New York, NY: Routledge.

WORKSHEET 3.1 ■ Working the Marble: Mix and Match the Anatomy

Take a stab at your paradigm. Consider the implications for your interrogative, topic, setting, perspectives, and tradition. Make varied combinations. Evaluate whether the combinations remain aligned. Consider possible answers and resultant research report genres. Revisit paradigm considerations. Mix and match the parts of the Anatomy until you generate research questions you want to pursue. You may need to make several copies of Worksheet 3.1. That's OK!

Paradigm	Interrogative	Substance (Topic)	Setting	Theoretical Perspective(s)	Tradition
Positivist Postpositivist Constructivist Critical Poststructuralist Other	Who What Where When Why How				Ethnography Phenomenology Narrative Inquiry Case Study Content Analysis Other
Option 1					
Option 2					

Option 3	
Option 4	
Option 5	
Option 6	

4 SAMPLE CONVERSATIONS: FORMULATING RESEARCH QUESTIONS

CHAPTER OUTLINE

Bert was a doctoral student in Natural Resources. He was interested in understanding urban green spaces. He was uncertain of his paradigm. He wondered whether research was worth doing if it lacked generalizability, a tenet of positivism. Susan was a doctoral student in nursing. She was concerned about the well-being of low socioeconomic status (SES) newborn babies when doctors recommended that mothers abandon breastfeeding for formula feeding. This chapter tells the stories of Bert and Susan as they peeled back the layers of their passions to craft viable research questions that could launch their research. These are composite stories, derived from hundreds of conversations, intended to demonstrate how you can begin with an idea (e.g., urban green spaces, feeding newborns) and use the Anatomy as a heuristic to transform your passions into actionable qualitative studies. The goal is to understand the backstory of how researchers can proceed from an idea to a research question that encapsulates all of the design elements of their study. Given such a question, you are poised to craft a rationale, identify related literature, position your methodology, and consider the genre of your research report. In other words, when you craft a robust research question that includes the parts of the Anatomy with all parts aligned, you will be ready to write a proposal (see Chapter 5).

BERT: URBAN GREEN SPACES

Bert knew he was interested in understanding urban green spaces. In his graduate course work and professional experiences, he was aware of efforts to convert vacant urban lots to green spaces such as vegetable gardens, flower gardens, or simply play spaces. These efforts were being funded by the government but he wondered if there was buy-in from the people who lived in these areas. While well intentioned, he wondered if these were top-down initiatives that would go awry without input from those they were intended to benefit. Initially, Bert thought a survey study would help him understand the general sentiments of those who lived in neighborhoods where urban green spaces might be created. He thought about the genre of the resultant report and wondered if a survey study could provide the insights he thought were needed. Then, he signed up for my section of Qualitative Research Methods.

The Anatomy in Action: Bert's Decision Process

As you might infer from the existence and structure of this book, I begin qualitative research courses with the role of paradigms. When Bert was in my class, we read about and discussed positivism, postpositivism, constructivism, criticalism, and poststructuralism. We considered alternate representations of paradigms and invited the class to explore transformative, emancipatory, postcolonial, indigenous, and pragmatic concepts. Bert realized that survey studies are a good fit for positivism and postpositivism. This realization provided a significant aha for him! He recognized that he was dissatisfied with the potential resulting report of a survey because, for him, such reports fell short of examining reality. He was unsure of his paradigm but knew that survey results rang hollow for him. He began to rephrase his topic according to paradigms and traditions.

I encouraged Bert to fill out Worksheet 3.1 (see Table 4.1). We could create multiple versions of his study. We could rework and reformulate until his question represented what he wanted to pursue. While filling out Option 1, he realized his real interest was about the wildlife in vacant lots and urban green spaces and the opinions the neighbors had about this wildlife. When asked what perspective he would take toward understanding wildlife, he was uncertain. He brainstormed varied theoretical perspectives used in his field: resilience, environmental conservation, socioecology, common-pool resources. To complete Option 1, Bert decided to consider the affordances (features, uses, potential) of ethnography. He pictured himself conducting work similar to Jane Goodall—instead of hanging out in Tanzania to understand

TABLE 4.1 ■ Working the Marble: Urban Green Spaces

Paradigm	Interrogative	Substance (Topic)	Setting	Theoretical Perspective(s)	Tradition
Option 1					
Postpositivist	What	Wildlife and wildlife habitat	Urban vacant lot	Resilience, Environmental Conservation, Socioecology, Common-pool resource	Ethnography
Option 2					
Constructivist	What	Neighbors' recommendations	Vacant lot neighborhood(s)	Common-pool resource	Case Study
Option 3					
Constructivist	What	Lived experiences with wildlife	Urban vacant lot neighbors	Common-pool resource	Phenomenology
Option 4					
Constructivist	What	Origins of wildlife perceptions	Urban vacant lot neighbors	Common-pool resource	Grounded Theory
Option 5					
Constructivist	What	Lived experiences with wildlife	Urban green space neighbors	Common-pool resource	Phenomenology

the culture of chimpanzees, he would hang out in a vacant lot. He would document the wildlife he observed as well as the responses that neighbors had to the wildlife. Paradigmatically, he considered whether his view of reality was represented by postpositivism: reality is expansive; systematic analyses facilitate the ability to make estimations of reality; the researcher and researched cannot be isolated therefore researcher bias must be acknowledged; findings are contextual and therefore not generalizable but may be transferable. These made sense to him. He was comfortable with framing his question as a postpositivist. He picked a perspective: common-pool resource theory. Option 1 resulted in the following question:

> *Given a postpositivist paradigm, what wildlife & wildlife habitats exist in an urban vacant lot from a common-pool resource perspective using ethnographic research methods?*

We started to tease out his topic. In Option 1, he targeted wildlife. However, his passion included neighbors' perceptions of wildlife. This cast doubt on the adequacy of Option 1. He then considered the implications of using ethnographic research methods. If he wanted to do an ethnography about wildlife in urban settings, he would need to be unobtrusive so that wildlife would be unhindered. He wondered whether he could avoid changing the normal behaviors of wildlife. He again considered his Option 1 topic: wildlife. He was interested in what the neighbors thought about the wildlife they encountered in urban vacant lots. He valued the neighbors' insights.

For Option 2, Bert considered whether his paradigmatic views of reality were postpositivistic. Because his passion was to understand the participants' reality, he wondered if he was paradigmatically a constructivist. So, he drafted Option 2.

> *Given a constructivist paradigm, what are the neighbors' wildlife recommendations who live near urban vacant lots from a common-pool resource perspective using case study methods?*

Bert valued what the people who lived near vacant lots thought about wildlife. He realized that he believed everyone constructs their own reality. Thus, those who live near vacant lots have varied realities as do those, like himself and possibly the policymakers funding these projects, have varied realities. He liked the idea of conducting research that would help him and policymakers understand the neighbors' realities and recommendations. This paradigmatic shift seemed like a good fit. He realized his topic was not wildlife but neighbors' recommendations regarding wildlife in nearby vacant lot(s). He decided to mull over the affordances of case study research methods. However, as he considered the purpose of case studies, he realized this research tradition would be inadequate. He was dissatisfied with the voice of participants in a case study report. He really wanted to conduct research that focused on participants' recommendations. Bert rolled the dice and drafted Option 3. According to Table 3.1, phenomenology is a research tradition honed to ascertain the lived experience of a phenomena. He thought that phenomenology may be a good fit for his purposes and wrote:

> *Given a constructivist paradigm, what are vacant urban lot neighbors' lived experiences with wildlife from a common-pool resource perspective using phenomenological research methods?*

He sat back to consider Option 3. Did he envision the data collection and analysis methods of a phenomenology as viable strategies to address his interests? Based on Seidman (2019), he wondered if he could logistically recruit participants who would spend 60–90 minutes with him every 3–5 days for 3 interview sessions. Logistical concerns are important. If you lack the resources (e.g., time, monies) to conduct the study, it behooves you to either garner the requisite resources or shift your research design.

Next, Bert wondered about the affordances of grounded theory. According to Table 3.1, grounded theory is a research tradition with the expressed purpose of generating a theory to explain the origins and predict the future of a topic. Ultimately, he wanted to generate a theory that explained the origins of wildlife perceptions that might predict the direction of wildlife perceptions. He formulated Option 4:

> *Given a constructivist paradigm, what are the origins of vacant lot neighbors' perceptions of wildlife from a common-pool resource perspective using grounded theory research methods?*

He decided that Option 4 was probably where he wanted to go with this line of research. However, he noted that without an understanding of the participants' lived experience he was unable to generate a grounded theory. Bert concluded he should first conduct a phenomenology and then see whether a grounded theory study would be a useful follow-up.

At this point, Bert remained dissatisfied with the setting. Was he interested in the lived experiences with wildlife among urban vacant lot neighbors or the lived experiences with wildlife among green space neighbors? He wrote Option 5:

> *Given a constructivist paradigm, what are urban green space neighbors' lived experiences with wildlife from a common-pool resource perspective using phenomenological research methods?*

Bert concluded that he was interested in neighbors' experiences with wildlife in urban vacant lots as well as urban green spaces. He simply needed to pick one and begin his first phenomenology. He could then proceed to his second phenomenology with the hopes of making headway toward a grounded theory study.

Throughout Bert's brainstorming and revisions (Options 1–5), two parts of the anatomy remained constant: the interrogative and his perspective. He quickly considered other interrogatives, *Who, Where, When, How,* and *Why* but determined that his overarching research question was aligned with understanding *What.* He might uncover *Who, Where, When, How,* and *Why* during his study but the essence of his study was to understand *What.* His research report would answer, *What* are the lived experiences? For Option 1, he listed several possible theoretical perspectives but quickly determined that common-pool resource theory was most useful to him. It is likely that while he hones his proposal, examines related literature, and conducts his first phenomenology, he may identify other or additional theories that help him collect and analyze his data. Such shifts are typical and should be embraced.

Affordances of the Anatomy: Bert's Process

Looking back at Bert's decisions listed in Table 4.1, we can see how an exploration of paradigms helped him hone in on his passion for participants' realities. By considering the tenets of postpositivism and the ensuing focus of the study, he was dissatisfied. He wrestled with this dissatisfaction which helped him realize that he deeply cared about the participants' viewpoint. When he considered the assumptions of constructivism, it made more sense that he was passionate about capturing the realities of urban neighbors. Contemplation of his paradigm facilitated not only his ability to refine his topic but also his research methods.

Returning to Table 4.1, we can see how Bert refined his topic by simultaneously considering his paradigm and the affordances of varied research traditions. Specifically, his topic went from *wildlife and wildlife habitats* to *neighbors' recommendations* to *lived experiences with wildlife* to the *origins of wildlife perceptions* and back to *lived experiences with wildlife*. In this process, he determined a trajectory for his work. He would begin with a phenomenology focused on neighbors' lived experience of urban green spaces. He would then conduct another phenomenology focused on neighbors' lived experience of urban vacant lots. Given these two studies, he would consider his preparedness to conduct a grounded theory study to generate a theory that explained the origins of participants' lived experiences and might shed light on the directions of participants' lived experiences. He had identified a research trajectory for the next several years. One study for his dissertation and additional studies to launch his career.

Using the Anatomy to refine his overarching research question helped Bert avoid much gnashing of teeth and heartache. If Bert had proceeded with Option 1, he would have spent invaluable time and resources to find and synthesize related literature focused on wildlife and wildlife habitats. If he had proceeded with Options 2 or 4, he would have spent invaluable time and resources to find and synthesize related literature focused on neighbors' recommendations for vacant lots or urban green spaces. Because Bert took the time to craft his research question, he was poised to find and synthesize related literature regarding lived experiences with wildlife. It is possible that while he seeks out related literature, he will be able to refine his topic even more. Hopefully, using the Anatomy helped him to at least head down a productive path and avoid dead ends and mountains of literature that fail to advance his research.

In addition, using the Anatomy helped Bert to refine not only his topic but also his research methods. Instead of designing an ethnography and then discarding the work necessary to design, propose, and initiate an ethnography—or even worse, conducting an ethnography only to find that he was dissatisfied with the findings, Bert was able to consider and similarly dismiss case study methods as well as grounded theory methods. Using the Anatomy, Bert honed his topic and selected a research tradition that would help him answer his question.

SUSAN: FEEDING NEWBORNS

As a doctoral student in nursing, Susan knew she was interested in a phenomenon she had frequently observed: doctors recommending to low SES mothers that they switch from breast to formula feeding. She strongly disagreed with this recommendation and therefore wanted to examine the topic. She wasn't interested in collecting babies' medical records to ascertain their health before and after switching to formula feeding. She really wanted to understand the mothers' perceptions of switching to formula. She wondered if they were being coerced.

The Anatomy in Action: Susan's Decision Process

Given a basic understanding of qualitative research traditions as described in Chapter 3, Susan thought her passion was a good fit with phenomenology. After all, she was interested in the mothers' lived experiences. Being familiar with the Anatomy and the Sample Question, Susan drafted Option 1,

> *Given a TBD paradigm, what is the lived experience of being told by your doctor to switch from breast to formula feeding using phenomenological research methods?*

She made a list of the parts of the Anatomy and filled out how Option 1 filled each slot:

1. Research paradigm: TBD
2. Interrogative: What
3. Substance or Topic: Lived experience
4. Setting/Parameters: Being told by doctor to switch from breast to formula feeding
5. Perspective: TBD
6. Research tradition: Phenomenological research methods

Susan came to class with Option 1 and asked her classmates for feedback. They wondered if the topic and parameters were parsed correctly. Would she collect and analyze data about lived experience? They wondered, lived experience of what? Susan revised her topic. Option 2 stated that her topic was the lived experience of being told and her setting/parameters was among mothers who switched from breast to formula feeding. However, Susan felt this phrasing moved away from her passion. She didn't want to understand the lived experience of being told, nor did she want to focus on whether mothers had actually switched. She was stymied. Classmates proposed that her actual topic was coercion. She wanted to study the lived experience of coercion. In this case, Option 3 became:

1. Research paradigm: TBD
2. Interrogative: What
3. Substance or Topic: Lived experience of coercion
4. Setting/Parameters: Among mothers who are told by their doctor to switch from breast to formula feeding
5. Perspective: TBD
6. Research tradition: Phenomenological research methods

This was a eureka moment! Parsing her passion so that she could understand that her focus was on coercion changed everything! Now she could search for related literature on coercion and extend the research that had been conducted on coercion. Before discussing Option 1 with her classmates, Susan was poised to find and read research about breast and formula feeding. While this remained a construct in her work (e.g., parameters), her focus on coercion untangled what had been a can of worms for her.

Next, Susan filled out Worksheet 3.1 (see Table 4.2) and noted that she needed to explore her paradigmatic assumptions. Given Option 3, Susan was able to ascertain that she was not a positivist. She was not interested in pre-/posttest data. She believed reality resided in the mothers. She was comfortable with the epistemological and ontological considerations of constructivism: Reality is ascribed by the human experience. In her case, she valued the lived experience of mothers. So far, she had identified her paradigm, interrogative, topic, setting/lived experience, and tradition. She needed to identify her theoretical perspective(s). She considered sociocultural theory, but her classmates told her they thought she was interested in whether the mothers were being disenfranchised. They thought her worldview was critical and she should consider theoretical perspective(s) such as feminism, identity theory, Marxism, postcolonialism, humanism, among varied perspectives that align with power. Susan insisted she was not a critical theorist. While she was interested in coercion and disenfranchisement as a topic, she did not believe her view of reality was paradigmatically critical. During her explorations of paradigms, she had determined that her worldview aligned with constructivism. Nonetheless, given the shift in her topic from lived experience to lived experience of coercion, she could see how feminist theories could inform her work.

The primary data set for phenomenological studies is typically in-depth interviews. The interviewer purposely invokes data collection and analysis strategies to glean the lived experience of the participants—not the researcher or the researcher's opinions of the topic. In Susan's case, she had definite opinions about mothers being told to switch from breast to formula feeding—she believed the mothers experienced coercion. She and her classmates wondered if she could conduct nonleading interviews. So, she decided to pilot her interview methods. She conducted initial interviews with a couple of mothers who fit her parameters. She then transcribed the interviews and brought the transcriptions to class. She asked classmates to evaluate the follow-up questions she used during the interviews. Did they tip her hat? Did the mothers fulfill the Pygmalion Effect by giving her the answers they detected she wanted to hear? In analysis of her transcripts, the classmates highlighted leading questions that

TABLE 4.2 ■ Working the Marble: Feeding Newborns

Paradigm	Interrogative	Substance (Topic)	Setting/Parameters	Theoretical Perspective(s)	Tradition
Option 1					
TBD	What	Lived experience	Being told by doctor to switch from breast to formula feeding	TBD	Phenomenology
Option 2					
TBD	What	Lived experience of being told	Mothers who switched from breast to formula feeding	TBD	Phenomenology
Option 3					
Constructivism	What	Lived experience of coercion	Mothers who are told by their doctor to switch from breast to formula feeding	Sociocultural	Phenomenology

Option 4					
Critical	What	Lived experience of coercion	Mothers who are told by their doctor to switch from breast to formula feeding	Feminist	Phenomenology
Option 5					
Critical	What	Lived experience of being advised by a doctor to switch to formula feeding	Mothers who were advised by a doctor to switch from breast to formula feeding	Coercion	Narrative inquiry
Option 6					
Constructivist	What	Stories	Mothers who are breast feeding	Coercion	Narrative inquiry

Susan unintentionally yet consistently used. She was so vested in her topic that she was unaware of ways she shared her bias with participants. Susan began to wonder whether she was indeed paradigmatically critical. She wrote Option 4,

> *Given a critical paradigm, what is the lived experience of coercion among mothers who are told by their doctor to switch from breast to formula feeding from a feminist perspective using phenomenological research methods?*

Seeing Option 4 on paper made her wonder whether phenomenology was a good fit after all. Because phenomenology typically seeks to limit bias maybe she should argue for a revised version of phenomenology which embraces researcher bias. Maybe she should explain the shortcomings of the tradition and formulate a critical phenomenology tradition. If coercion were her topic, maybe she needed to revise her parameters from, mothers being told to switch, to simply, mothers of newborns. This shift omitted the recommendations of doctors to switch to formula but centered on the lived experience of coercion. Conducting a phenomenology about coercion, where she targeted coercion, would mean she could be transparent and forthright to ask participants about coercion.

Before formulating a new research tradition or shifting her topic, Susan pondered other traditions and decided to explore narrative inquiry as a possible fit for her passion. She understood that narrative inquiry valued the stories of the participants while including the researcher as part of the story. In other words, if she used narrative inquiry research methods, she could be transparent throughout her data collection and analysis that she thought doctors' advice to switch from breast to formula feeding was coercive. She could tell participants' stories through her lens of coercion. She then realized that coercion may actually be her theoretical lens instead of her topic. She wrote Option 5,

> *Given a critical paradigm, what is the lived experience of being advised to switch from breast to formula feeding from a coercion perspective using narrative inquiry research methods?*

Seeing Option 5 on paper, she realized that with narrative inquiry her topic would shift from lived experience of a phenomena to participants' stories. She remained convinced that she was paradigmatically a constructivist. Susan wrote Option 6,

> *Given a constructivist paradigm, what are the stories of mothers who have been advised to switch from breast to formula feeding from a coercion perspective using narrative inquiry research methods?*

Option 6 was a relief! She felt this articulated her passion while allowing her to be true to her concern that mothers were being coerced and adhered to her worldview, constructivism. She was thrilled to learn that a constructivist could be passionate about power and take a power-based perspective. It is possible that she will find additional power-focused theories (e.g., feminism, post-colonialism, posthumanism) to be useful and may incorporate them as well. Susan was eager to find out whether her concerns were held by the participants. Using narrative inquiry, she could tell her story alongside her participants'. Susan decided to design a study based on Option 6.

Affordances of the Anatomy: Susan's Process

Susan initiated her quest to formulate a viable research question with confidence in her passion: she wanted to understand the coercion that mothers experienced when doctors advised them to switch from breast to formula feeding. As a nurse, she was concerned that mothers were intimidated at worst or simply deferred to their doctors without considering the options or ramifications at best. The Anatomy gave her some structure to translate her interests into a research question. Option 1 helped to put her passion on paper. She could see the need to specify her paradigm as well as her theoretical perspective(s). Meanwhile, she could ask classmates for feedback. They quickly noted that she had parsed the question incorrectly. The Anatomy helped her reparse from "lived experience" to "lived experience of coercion."

Returning to the blank spots on the Anatomy, Susan wondered about her theoretical perspective(s). Without the Anatomy, she may have proceeded without understanding her theoretical perspective. After all, she was fairly settled on her paradigm, interrogative, topic, setting/parameters, and research tradition. Indeed, she may have been able to collect and analyze data. However, without thinking through her theoretical lens before she designed the study, she would have encountered difficulty when she needed to determine what "counted" as data. When you conduct qualitative research, you must define what you deem as data. Your perspective helps you ascertain what are data for your study and what are not. Susan will make assumptions when she defines her unit of data. These assumptions are rooted in theory—whether she knows it or not. If she had not identified her lens at this point, she may have had to shift her study or possibly start over. Finally, without purposely and strategically collecting and analyzing data with specified theoretical assumptions, she would be hard-pressed to discuss the significance of her work. Due to the Anatomy, she considered whether coercion was informed by sociocultural or feminist theories. At some point, these theoretical considerations gave her another aha! Maybe coercion wasn't her topic but her lens! Maybe she viewed advice given by doctors through a coercion lens. Without the Anatomy, she may have gone forward with coercion as her topic.

By recognizing her theoretical perspective, Susan was able to return to her original conviction: she was paradigmatically a constructivist. While constructivism and phenomenology are a good fit, she was wise to pilot her phenomenological research methods. When her peers were able to identify leading questions, she revisited her research tradition and identified narrative inquiry as a possible fit. This resulted in one final revision to her topic.

Using the Anatomy proved invaluable to Susan as she transformed her passion into an actionable qualitative research question. If Susan had proceeded with Option 1, she would have been lost. Her topic was ill-defined as a lived experience. Her setting/parameters was not her actual arena of interest. Her research methods would have chaffed as she attempted to limit her perspective while collecting interview data. By filling out the Anatomy, Susan was able to move the pieces of her question around until they fit into their rightful places. She made substitutions, considered corresponding findings as well as the report genre, and revisited paradigmatic tenets. Susan's progression through Options 1–6 involved "working the marble." She got the parts out on the table when she wrote Option 1. When she filled the empty slots, she was forced to revise the other slots. Coercion moved from her setting/parameters to her topic to her lens. Due to her interest in coercion, she evaluated her worldview; she wondered if she was paradigmatically critical. When she realized she could be a constructivist who took power-oriented perspectives (e.g., coercion, feminism, Marxism, posthumanism) while collecting and analyzing data, she was relieved and ready to formulate a study that targeted her interests while remaining true to her worldview.

CHAPTER SUMMARY

I had a colleague who reminisced that at her own dissertation defense, her committee congratulated her on conducting a methodologically solid research study. She had collected and analyzed data as proposed and had done her work well. However, they wondered whether she has actually answered her research question. Only then did she realize she was answering a different question than she had proposed. Thankfully, the question she actually answered was her true passion—so it all worked out. Given the Anatomy, hopefully, you can avoid this scenario. By working through the Anatomy, Bert and Susan formulated solid qualitative research questions and were poised to find related literature, articulate their research-based rationales, identify their research methods as well as write corresponding research reports.

Chapter 4 described Bert and Susan's use of the Anatomy to refine their research question. By considering varied paradigms, interrogatives, perspectives, traditions and genres, they were able to hone their topics and settings/parameters. They avoided dead ends as they proceeded to synthesize related literature. Given honed research questions, they are poised to write a rational and propose their studies. They are ready for Chapter 5.

5 PROCEED FROM QUESTION TO PROPOSAL

CHAPTER OUTLINE

Innovative vs Significant Research
- Using the Anatomy as a Heuristic for Innovation
- In Pursuit of Significance

Rationales, Conceptual Frameworks, and Methodologies
- Rationale: Sell Your Idea
- Conceptual Framework: Where Significance Resides
- Theoretical Perspective(s): Move the Proverbial Tablecloth
- Related Literature of Substantive Constructs
- Methodology: Explain the Fit
- Methods: Critique Trustworthiness
- Logistics: Gatekeepers, Timelines, Phases, and Budget

Welcome to a New Frontier: Summary and Conclusion
- Suggested Activities and Discussions
- Suggested Resources
- Worksheet 5.1: Examine Innovation and Significance
- Worksheet 5.2: Proposal Worksheet
- Worksheet 5.3: Trustworthiness

In Chapter 1, I introduced a six-part heuristic that can be used to draft and revise qualitative research questions. I refer to this heuristic as the Anatomy of a Qualitative Research Question. I examined a sample question and deconstructed it according to this heuristic. Next, I used the Anatomy to examine a seminal study. In Chapter 2, I asserted that we conduct research to grapple with truth and to make sense of reality. However, researchers differ in their understanding of truth and reality. These varied understandings are known as paradigms. I challenged the notion that research begins by asking a research question and then determining whether the question is best answered with quantitative or qualitative research methods. Rather, researchers ask the questions they ask because they have deeply held paradigmatic convictions. Thus, Chapter 2 was an admonition to begin your research by understanding your own paradigm. Introduced to a heuristic for formulating qualitative research questions, the deconstruction of a sample qualitative research question and analysis of seminal studies using the Anatomy (Chapter 1) as well as an introduction to paradigms and their role in crafting research (Chapter 2), in Chapter 3, I proposed metacognitive strategies for embracing your passions to craft your own research questions. In Chapter 4, I contextualized the Anatomy and metacognitive strategies by telling the composite stories of Bert and Susan as they used the Anatomy to brainstorm, draft, revise, brainstorm some more, revise some more, and eventually craft viable qualitative research questions. Using the Anatomy, their questions entail the basic components of qualitative research design. They are poised to proceed from well-designed questions to full-blown research proposals. This is where Chapter 5 picks up the process.

In this chapter, I first compare innovation and significance. Typically, research contributes to current notions of your topic, theories, paradigms, and research methods. Research strives to push our current conceptualizations forward. In other words, research seeks to be significant. I therefore begin Chapter 5 by encouraging you to critique your question for significance. Next, I turn to how you can use your Anatomy-based question to formulate a rationale, identify the constructs of your **conceptual framework** (constructs of your theoretical perspective(s) and substantive tenets which provide the topics of your related literature) and thereby strategically examine related literature, revisit the fit between the parts of your question, and critique the trustworthiness of your research methods. I am hopeful that by the end of Chapter 5, you will be prepared to write your proposal and pursue your research passions.

INNOVATIVE VS SIGNIFICANT RESEARCH

Using the Anatomy as a Heuristic for Innovation

It has been said that innovation occurs at the intersection of previously unrelated concepts (e.g., Einstein, 1982). When you intersect roller skates with ice skates, you create roller blades. When you intersect sailing with surfing, you get windsurfing. We can purposely create intersections of previously unrelated concepts. We can be innovative on purpose. If you want to be innovative, create the intersection of previously unrelated concepts. As such, the Anatomy can be used heuristically to deliberately ask innovative research questions. For example, you can purposely intersect previously unrelated theoretical perspectives with a topic of research, a topic of research with a new research tradition, or a topic of research with a new setting. If previous studies in your field have examined your topic using Theoretical Perspective X, you can contribute to your field by asking about your topic using Theoretical Perspective Y. If previous studies in your field have examined your topic in Setting A, you can be innovative by conducting your study in Setting B. If previous studies in your field have examined your topic using research traditions Q, you can be innovative by using research tradition R.

If you are formulating your own research question as you read this book, by the end of Chapter 4, using varied substitutions, you aligned the parts of the Anatomy, pondered hypothetical answers, and considered your desired report genre. You can now use the Anatomy to consider the innovativeness of your question. For example, in Table 5.1, I compare hypothetically related literature to the sample question. I specify the paradigm, interrogative, setting, perspective(s), and research tradition used in each study. In this brief hypothetical analysis, you can see that *What* is a common interrogative, the topic shifts, the settings shift, the perspectives tend to invoke varied mixes of cognitive and sociocultural perspectives, and the traditions all differ. The sample question builds on the related literature by shifting the topic, setting, and tradition. In other words, the sample question is unlike previous studies by purposely intersecting previously isolated topic, setting, and tradition. Using the Anatomy as a heuristic for innovation, you are poised to articulate how your work builds on and extends related literature.

To ask innovative questions, systematically and explicitly analyze the related literature according to the Anatomy to make decisions that purposely intersect previously isolated concepts. Use Worksheet 5.1 to evaluate the literature that is related to your study.

In Pursuit of Significance

I want to quickly point out distinctions between innovation and significance. Just because you ask an innovative question doesn't mean that it is significant. One reason to conduct research is to provide significant insights that unveil important truths and new insights. While innovation cannot be equated with significance, I propose that without innovation, your work may lack significance. In other words, I propose that significant questions are typically innovative but not all innovations are significant. While the intersection of

TABLE 5.1 ■ Using the Anatomy to Evaluate Related Literature and Ask Innovative Questions

Topic: Integration of Literacy and Technology				
	Jones (2017)	Smith (2018)	Johnson (2019)	Sample
Paradigm	Constructivist	Positivist	Constructivist	Postpositivist
Interrogative	What	What	How	What
Topic	Lived experience of using social media	Reading comprehension	Engage in Language Experience	Nature of Literacy
Setting	Not applicable	Controlled online inquiry software	Online narrative gaming	Technology-rich fourth-grade classroom
Perspective(s)	Sociocognitive	Cognitive	Sociocultural	Sociocultural
Tradition	Phenomenology	Quantitative	Case Study	Ethnography

chocolate with peanut butter may be significant (especially for all Reese's lovers) the intersection of chocolate with mud is arguably insignificant. Millions of questions are asked every day but relatively few are significant. Innovation may open the doors for significance but certainly doesn't guarantee significance. While the Anatomy may help you formulate a research question that embodies a corresponding design framework, and even provide an intentional strategy for asking innovative questions, the Anatomy does not guarantee that you will ask a significant question. Thus, using the Anatomy as a heuristic for innovation is an important but not a final step.

The consistent and persistent question posed by my doctoral advisor at the end of conversations about my sundry dissertation ideas was: So what? Why should anyone care? This question always stopped me in my tracks but remains a pivotal point as I design research. My advisor challenged me to articulate the significance of my research question. Why expend extraordinary amounts of time, energy, and resources in pursuit of conducting a study that I cannot defend as significant? If you cannot give a strong argument for significance, it is time to ditch your research question and go back to the drawing board. Save yourself from wasting time, energy, and resources! You may lament the loss of your question but because you used the Anatomy, you are positioned to strategically think through your next question. You will have refined your interests, considered your paradigm, explored useful theoretical perspectives, and evaluated research traditions with their corresponding report genres. You will be poised to animate the Anatomy as you formulate a new research question.

RATIONALES, CONCEPTUAL FRAMEWORKS, AND METHODOLOGIES

Table 5.2 provides a common outline for qualitative research proposals. Qualitative research proposals are a genre. Just as jazz music is distinctive from rap music and mystery novels are distinctive from historical fiction novels, so too are research proposals distinctive from varied forms of writing. There are common elements. Like any genre, artistry is also involved. So, while Table 5.2 details common elements, the artistry you bring to your proposal is welcome and varied. In addition, the parameters of a proposal requested by your doctoral committee, designed with colleagues, specified by funding agencies, and across diverse fields may differ from this outline. Nonetheless, the elements are fairly consistent.

The Anatomy can help you formulate your rationale as well as parse down the constructs for your conceptual framework. Just as there is reciprocity

TABLE 5.2 ■ Sample Qualitative Proposal Outline

I. Rationale, Question, and/or Purpose Statement
II. Conceptual Framework of Related Literature
   A. Theoretical Perspective(s)
   B. Substantive Constructs

III. Methodology
   A. Paradigm
      i. State and Define Paradigm
      ii. Compare Types and Tenets within your paradigm
      iii. Situate yourself within your paradigm
      iv. Explain the fit between your paradigm and your research question

   B. Research Tradition
      i. Define Tradition
         Note: If Traditions are inadequate, explain and propose amalgamation/innovation
      ii. Explain the fit between your research tradition and question
      iii. Setting, Participants, and Role of Researcher
      iv. Data Sources and Collection Methods
      v. Data Analysis Methods
      vi. Trustworthiness

   C. Logistics
      i. Gatekeepers: IRB and Setting/Participants
      ii. Timeline
      iii. Budget

among the parts of the Anatomy whereby you revise and refine your research question as you substitute the parts, there is reciprocity between your rationale, conceptual framework, and methodology with your research question.

In other words, you may not be done with revising your research question. As you write your rationale, conceptual framework, and methodology, you may find additional ways to tighten your focus. Wonderful! The more you can refine and tighten before you collect and analyze data, the less you may get lost in the forest. Embrace these additional opportunities to nail down your interests. Like Michelangelo, keep chipping away.

In Table 5.3, I align the sample question (see Chapter 1), the parts of the anatomy (see Chapters 1–4), and a common proposal outline (see Table 5.2). Tables 5.2 and 5.3 give you the big picture for Chapter 5. As you read this chapter, attempt to fill out Worksheet 5.2.

TABLE 5.3 ■ Alignment Between Question, Anatomy, and Proposal Outline

Sample Research Question	Parts of the Anatomy	Proposal Outline
Given a postpositivist paradigm[1], what[2] is the nature of literacy[3] in a technology-rich fourth-grade classroom[4] from a sociocultural perspective[5] using ethnographic[6] research methods?	1. Research paradigm: Postpositivist 2. Interrogative: What 3. Substance or Topic: Nature of literacy 4. Setting: Technology-rich fourth-grade classroom 5. Perspective: Sociocultural 6. Research tradition: Ethnographic	I. Rationale, Question, and/or Purpose Statement II. Conceptual Framework of Related Literature A. Theoretical Perspective(s) B. Substantive Constructs III. Methodology A. Paradigm B. Research Tradition C. Logistics

Alignment

I. Rationale, Question and/or Purpose Statement
- Given A: #5 regarding #3
- Given B: #4
- = Question/Purpose #1–6
- NOTE: The order of your given statements may differ from the Sample.

II. Conceptual Framework of Related Literature
  A. Theoretical Perspective(s)
  - *#5 Perspective: Sociocultural*

  B. Substantive Constructs
  - *#4 Setting: Technological culture*
  - *#3 Topic: Nature of literacy*

(Continued)

TABLE 5.3 ■ Alignment Between Question, Anatomy, and Proposal Outline (Continued)

Sample Research Question	Parts of the Anatomy	Proposal Outline
III. Methodology A. Paradigm • *#1 Research paradigm: Postpositivist* B. Research Tradition • *#6 Research tradition: Ethnographic* • *#4 Setting: Technology-rich fourth-grade classroom* C. Logistics • *#4 Setting: Technology-rich fourth-grade classroom* • *#6 Research tradition: Ethnographic*		

Rationale: Sell Your Idea

Another advantage of using the Anatomy is the relative ease it provides for converting your question into a rationale (see Table 5.3). Rationales are sales pitches. Rationales are what songwriters might call a hook. Rationales should convince your audience, and yourself, that the question you propose is significant. I prefer to draft my rationale in terms of Given Statements that crescendo with a purpose statement or research question. In other words, I write out, Given A, Given B, Given C, therefore <insert purpose statement/ research question>. You may find anywhere from two to five Given Statements are useful. Make as many or few Given Statements as you need to conclude with a purpose statement/research question. To convert my research question into a rationale, I block out the parts of the Anatomy and convert them to Given Statements. I return to the Sample Research Question,

> *Given a postpositivist paradigm, what is the nature of literacy in a technology-rich fourth-grade classroom from a sociocultural perspective using ethnographic research methods?*

> Given A: The nature of literacy changes as culture changes (topic and perspective)
>
> Given B: We live in a technological culture (setting)
>
> Question: What is the nature of literacy in our technological culture? (After IRB approval as well as gate keeper and participant consent, the setting was refined to a technology-rich fourth-grade classroom).

In this example, the Given Statements refer to the topic, perspective, and setting. They omit the paradigm and research tradition. For the purpose of crafting your rationale, this is intentional. The topic, perspective, and setting become parts of the Conceptual Framework (discussed below) while the paradigm and research tradition become part of the Methodology (see below). NOTE: It is possible that the reason you are conducting your study is because you bring fresh paradigmatic view of research traditions to the examination of your topic. In which case, paradigm and methods would be part of your rationale.

Wolcott (2009) recommends that qualitative writers begin proposals and reports with a purpose statement. I find that this recommendation is often useful and makes the purpose of the research obvious to readers and the researcher. However, there are times that it makes sense to conclude the rationale with your purpose statement/research question. Whether you are writing a proposal or a final report, consider making your purpose statement either the first line of your write up or the conclusion of your rationale. Play with your Given Statements. You may find that writing these statements helps you revise your research question. Great! The more you can hone your question before you start your study, the more focused you can be as you begin data collection and analysis.

Some refer to rationales as elevator speeches. I like the concept. Can you pitch your study within the timeframe of an elevator ride? Within 1–2 minutes, can you convince colleagues, family, and friends why you plan to conduct your study? When I teach qualitative research methods courses, I ask doctoral students to get into two concentric circles. I give them 1–2 minutes to express their rationale and then shift to the next person and try it again. I find that multiple opportunities to express their rationale helps them refine their sales pitch by revising their Given Statements. Then, I ask them to debrief with those who heard their pitches. Such debriefing can facilitate continued revisions to the Given Statements as well as provide valuable insights about the expectations their audience developed for the study.

I find that researchers are commonly too close to their own work to grasp the expectations their audience may have for their work. For example, during my elevator speech, I may say that my work is focused on the Nature of Literacy but my audience may expect me to report the impact of using technology on students' literacy development. In other words, my sales pitch failed to help my audience understand *Nature of Literacy* as a topic. Insights into what my audience expects can help me identify *what my study is NOT about*. These are the **delimitations** of my study. Sometimes I learn about the delimitations of my study when I receive reviews. Comments might be made that have little to do with the focus of the study. I then realize that I need to specify, for my audience and myself, not only what my study is about but also what it is not about. Identifying your delimitations can help you as you turn from your rationale to your conceptual framework. Understanding your delimitations can minimize meandering into tangentially related theoretical perspectives and related literature and thereby save you valuable time, resources, and energy.

Conceptual Framework: Where Significance Resides

Conceptual Frameworks (CFs) consist of literature related to two components: (1) theoretical perspective(s) and (2) substantive constructs. Your CF is the backbone of your study. This is where you establish the precipice of work done in your field as it relates to your theoretical perspective(s) and substantive constructs. The more robust your CF, the more fodder you have for a discussion of your findings. The significance of your work resides in using your CF to discuss your findings. In the sample question and corresponding rationale, the CF consists of a sociocultural perspective and the nature of literacy. Many qualitative research traditions' code for emergent findings and therefore the related literature may shift during the study. In other words, the constructs you started with may not fully capture the constructs that your emergent findings can be compared to. If this is the case, then the CF constructs of your proposal may differ from the constructs in your final write-ups. Regardless, your ability to compare and contrast your work with those who have gone before you is where significance resides. I commend Table 5.1 and Worksheet 5.1 to support your discussion of significance both in your proposal as well as final reports.

Theoretical Perspective(s): Move the Proverbial Tablecloth

I find that it can be useful to begin a discussion of your conceptual frameworks with your theoretical perspective(s) because they have implications for how you view the related literature. In the sample, I take one perspective, sociocultural. I therefore begin the conceptual framework by defining sociocultural theory and how it has informed current conceptions of the nature of literacy and why it is useful to the study at hand. The goal is to explain to your audience how your lens frames your work. Depending on your field, it may be important to discuss the spectrum of perspectives commonly used (which may extend beyond the perspectives you plan to use) or the spectrum within the perspective(s) you plan to take. Describe where your work resides in the spectrum and why you chose the theoretical tenets that you chose. Who else takes these perspectives? How do your perspectives build on others' perspectives? How do your perspectives differ? If applicable, how might your work extend the theoretical perspectives commonly used in your field? How might your work extend the theoretical perspective(s) regardless of field? As described in Chapter 1, I metaphorically consider theoretical perspectives as comparable to a tablecloth. If your work can shift basic theoretical assumptions, then your work can shift all constructs built on that theory. You may wonder if you have a theoretical perspective. You may be tempted to skip or skimp on this part of your CF. I assure you, yes, you have theoretical assumptions about your topic. Unpack your tacit assumptions. Make them explicit so you can pull the proverbial tablecloth. (For strategies to unearth your perspective(s), see Chapter 3, *Substitute the Theoretical Perspective(s).*)

It is possible that the purpose of your study is to examine a theoretical framework. For example, I worked with an insightful doctoral student who crafted a robust research question to examine the lived experience of teachers who work in Waldorf Schools. She deftly articulated the anthroposophy philosophy of Waldorf Schools but hadn't considered her own theoretical stance toward anthroposophy. In other words, her topic was the lived experience of a philosophy. She needed to unpack her view of this philosophy. She needed to articulate the assumptions she held as she collected and analyzed her data. Remember, your theoretical perspective is what informs you throughout data collection and analysis. If you attend the State Fair as a child, your view of the fair differs from those who run a game booth (see Chapter 3: *Suggested Activities 4b*). If you hike up a mountain, the path you chose will change your view of the mountain. Your theoretical perspective informs what "counts" as data. If your topic consists entirely of theoretical constructs, be sure to include your perspective toward the theoretical framework.

Related Literature of Substantive Constructs

In the past, academia referred to literature reviews. I attempt to catch myself and refrain from using the term literature review because I think it is a misnomer. There was a time when researchers conducted an exhaustive review of the extant literature. In our current technological culture, we have access to a myriad of research literature and therefore identify and synthesize related literature—not to be confused with a comprehensive review of all studies ever conducted on the topic formerly known as a Literature Review.

The Anatomy can help you identify the constructs of your related literature. You can waste a lot of time by delving into literature that is tangentially related to your study. While you make substitutions to reformulate your research question, your topic and perspective(s) can shift. Accordingly, the constructs of your conceptual framework shift. In Chapter 4, I told the stories of Bert and Susan who used the Anatomy to refine their research questions. Bert's substantive constructs shifted from (1) *wildlife and wildlife habitats* to (2) *neighbors' recommendations* to (3) *lived experience with wildlife* to (4) *origins of wildlife perceptions* and back to (5) *lived experiences with wildlife*. Susan's substantive constructs evolved from (1) *lived experience* to (2) *lived experience of being told* to (3) *lived experience of coercion* to (4) *stories*. Each shift invoked different bodies of literature.

In the sample question, while refining my question, the *nature of literacy* came into focus as the topic of my study. Thus, I found literature that examined the basic components, characteristics, of the nature of reading and writing. I found seminal works in my field and described how those scholars depicted the nature of literacy. Due to my perspective (sociocultural) and setting (technology-rich), I found literature that examined the nature of literacy in technological settings. As described earlier, I could have lost my way if I had focused on tangential topics such as literacy acquisition, the impact of using technology on students' literacy development, and the pros and cons of integrating technology into a literacy curriculum, among a myriad of other options. Because I was aware of my perspective toward literacy (sociocultural), my topic (nature of literacy), and my setting (technology-rich classroom), I was able to resist spending valuable time exploring tangentially related albeit interesting topics.

Doctoral students often say to me the reason they are asking their question is because it has never been asked before. The purpose of doing research is to push current conceptions of reality to new realms. Thus, the "never done before" argument might be the rationale for every study. Does this mean there is no related literature? I have found that the "never done before" argument invites dissertation committees, journal reviewers, and funding agencies to ask the following questions: (1) is this person the smartest person we have ever encountered so as to come up with a question never asked or (2) has no one ever asked this question because it is worthless or (3) has this person not done their homework to ascertain what has already been done? I recommend that you avoid the "never done before" argument and instead describe how your work resides at a new intersection of substantive constructs.

At the beginning of this chapter, I described how innovation occurs at the intersection of previously unrelated concepts (e.g., the intersection of roller skates and ice skates becomes roller blades; the intersection of sailing and windsurfing becomes windsurfing). The previously unrelated concepts of your study become the constructs for your discussion of related literature. If I were pitching a study about roller blades, I might describe roller skates as well as ice skates. Given a thorough description of these constructs, I could provide a rationale for their intersection and explain why roller blades are needed. Your discussion of related literature may therefore describe previously unrelated topics. By completing Worksheet 5.1, you may be able to identify the related literature of the substantive constructs you need to discuss. It is true, unless you are replicating a study, your work is unique—never done before. Explain to your audience how it will extend the current theoretical and substantive concepts of previously unrelated constructs. Explain how the intersection of previously unrelated theoretical and/or substantive constructs is significant. Before windsurfing existed, you could have argued that it had never been done before. I would contend your argument, while true, would be inadequate. In reality, it is an extension of previously unrelated constructs. Instead of saying this work should be done because there is a vacuum, a better argument is to focus on a new intersection. Similarly, instead of arguing that no one has ever explored your topic, discuss the uniqueness of the intersection for your constructs.

Methodology: Explain the Fit

Some wonder about the difference between methodology and methods. **Methodology** *includes your paradigm and a discussion of the fit between your paradigm and methods*. Methods are simply how you collect and analyze data. Thus, methods are a subset of your methodology. Begin your Methodology chapter/section by stating and defining your paradigm. You might begin your Methodology chapter/section with something like: As a constructivist, I believe reality is ascribed by human experience. Proceed to elaborate on the tenets of your paradigm. If paradigms are new to you, it is time to delve deeper. For example, there are many types of constructivism. You need to explore the full range of constructivism and consider who you are among the variants. Explain whether you are a radical constructivist, social constructivist, or another type of constructivist. Explain how your epistemology and ontology compare with other constructivists. Do you agree or disagree with Bakhtin, Piaget, Von Glaserfeld, Vygotsky, and others? Place yourself among the spectrum of constructivist tenets. Situate yourself within the realm of constructivism. As a constructivist, contrast your view of reality with other constructivists.

After discussing your paradigm, remind your audience of your research question. Then, explain why a person with your paradigmatic assumptions would ask your research question (see Table 5.4). For example, returning to the sample question, as a postpositivist, I believe that reality is expansive and can be at best only estimated. The research question, therefore, considers the expansive reality of literacy by focusing on the nature, essence, of literacy.

The findings will be formulated in terms of 3–5 estimated characteristics of the nature of literacy. As a postpositivist, I believe that reality is context-specific. I therefore pose a question that is situated in a specific classroom for a specific duration and the findings will be contextualized within this time and space. In other words, prolonged (not to be confused with longitudinal) exposure to the setting will be necessary to provide a thick description of the setting. Only then might the findings transfer with the notation that reality is nongeneralizable.

TABLE 5.4 ■ Fit Between Paradigm, Question, and Tradition

Paradigm	Question	Tradition
Postpositivist	*Given a postpositivist paradigm, what is the nature of literacy in a technology-rich fourth-grade classroom from a sociocultural perspective using ethnographic research methods?*	Ethnography
• Reality is expansive • Systematic analyses facilitate the ability to make estimations of reality • The researcher and researched cannot be isolated, therefore researcher bias must be acknowledged • Findings are contextual and therefore not generalizable but may be transferable	• Expansive: Nature of literacy • Systematic: Describe 3–5 estimated characteristics that emerge from this setting • Contextual: Specific classroom for specific timeframe • Contextual: Prolonged engagement needed to describe context of findings for possible transfer • Bias: sociocultural view of literacy	• The study of ethos (culture at a specific time and place) is the definition of ethnography • Data collection and analyses are systematized • Role of the researcher is documented and reported as best as it can be • Researcher bias is part of proposal (e.g., sociocultural) as well as data collection and analysis (e.g., memos) • Thick description of the setting provides context for findings with possible transfer

Given your paradigm, a description of your epistemological and ontological beliefs, a restatement of your research question and why someone with your beliefs about reality would care about such a question, proceed to explain the fit between your question and research tradition. In the Sample Question, ethnography is a good fit for several reasons. Ethnography, by definition, is the study (*graphy*) of an ethos (*culture*). Culture is inherently bound by time and place and therefore aligns with notions of contextually bound realities. Ethnography is systematic so as to provide estimations of reality. Ethnographic research methods specify the importance of negotiations with gatekeepers as well as participants as the starting point for keeping note of the researcher's role in the study and how participants view the role of the researcher. Taking note of this role as it shifts and grows is part of ethnographic research methods. Researcher bias is initially expressed in the proposal in terms of theoretical perspective(s). During data collection, researcher bias is purposely noted in daily memos. Analyses of these memos is part of the final report with the goal of bias transparency. Finally, ethnographic research reports include thick descriptions of the setting so as to contextualize the findings. As a postpositivist, I would argue that only the readers can ascertain transfer from the research setting to their own. The report, therefore, provides extensive descriptions of the setting.

In summary, begin your Methodology section by defining and explaining the fit between your paradigm and your research question. Follow this up with an explanation of the fit between your research question and your research tradition. Then continue with the *Qualitative Proposal Outline* specified in Table 5.2. Specifically, proceed with a description of your role, the participants' role, and the proposed setting. Next, identify the sources of data (e.g., artifacts, interviews, observations) and how these data will be collected and analyzed. As specified in Chapter 3, you may need to propose a new tradition by describing the inadequacies of the current options and proposing data collection, data analysis, and a report genre that gel to address threats to trustworthiness. You may become the forerunner of a new research tradition! In-depth descriptions of data collection and analysis methods are not the purpose of this book. Rather, when you get to this point, I commend you to the vast wealth of books that are written about varied qualitative research traditions (see Chapter 3: *Suggested Readings).*

Methods: Critique Trustworthiness

As indicated in Table 5.2, the Research Tradition section of your research proposal should conclude with a robust plan for trustworthiness. Have you ever watched the video *Margaret Mead and Samoa*? When I teach qualitative research courses, I always begin the conversation about trustworthiness by watching this video. As you know, Margaret Mead is a renowned qualitative researcher. Her 1929 ethnographic dissertation and resultant book, *Coming of Age in Samoa*, catapulted her to fame. There remains a hall at the American Museum of Natural History in New York, where she worked from 1926 to 1978, that bears her name. The video is of interest because it features another researcher, Derek Freeman, who also conducted research in Samoa in the 1940s and 1960s. He claims that Margaret Mead's findings were inaccurate due to a lack of qualitative research rigor. In other words, Freeman believes that Mead's work is not trustworthy. I encourage you to go to YouTube and find this video (at the time of printing, see https://youtu.be/GOCYhmnx6o8). Discuss the implications for qualitative research design. My hope is to help you avoid the pitfalls of a poorly designed study that is decried for its lack of trustworthiness.

In Lincoln and Guba's (1985a, 1985b) seminal treaty for the viability of nonpositivistic qualitative research, they carefully mapped positivistic concerns for internal validity, external validity, reliability, and objectivity in terms of nonpositivistic criteria for trustworthiness which include credibility, transferability, dependability, and confirmability. The research tradition used to address the sample question was ethnography. Table 5.5 highlights the four criteria of trustworthiness for the sample question and lists the concerns related to each criterion that commonly arise when using ethnographic research methods. Finally, Table 5.5 identifies research methods that will be used in this study to purposely address each criterion and concern. Revisit the video about Margaret Mead. Examine her use of these criterion, concerns, and methods. Be sure to note that Mead's work was in the 1920s while Lincoln and Guba's explication of trustworthiness didn't occur until the 1980s. My goal is not to deride Mead's work but to point out that in the ensuing century methodologists recognized the need to undergird trustworthiness.

In Chapter 3, I leveraged the affordances of research traditions to refine my research question. I cycled through ethnography, phenomenology, case study, narrative inquiry, biography, grounded theory, and content analysis traditions. Another advantage to aligning your work with a research tradition is that threats to trustworthiness and methods to undergird trustworthiness are specified. You simply need to describe how these strategies will be used in your study. If you argue for an amalgamation of research traditions or the innovation of new research methods, you will need to ascertain how the trustworthiness of your study will be threatened and identify strategies to address each concern. Whether you plan to use an established tradition or propose new methods, go to Worksheet 5.3, and make plans for the trustworthiness of your study.

There are **limitations** (inadequacies) to all research designs. In other words, there is no such thing as the perfect research design. For example, the findings that emerged from the study conducted to address the sample question, with all the plans for trustworthiness, should be considered as one

TABLE 5.5 ■ Ethnographic Trustworthiness: Corresponding Criteria, Concerns, and Methods

Criteria	Concerns	Methods
Credibility *Truth value, capable of being believed*	• Learn the culture • Test for misinformation • Build trust • Identify salient elements • Identify crucial atypical events • Researcher bias • Human instrument frailty	• Prolonged period of participant observation • Triangulation of sources and methods • Peer debriefing • Negative case analysis • Member check • Constant Comparative Method • Estimations of data collection obtrusiveness
Transferability *Ability to infer implications from research to other settings*	• Provide reader with contextual reference	• Thick descriptions
Dependability *Used methods as specified*	• Methodological shifts • Establish redundancy • Pygmalion Effect • Hawthorne Effect • Inquirer sophistication	• Overlap of data collection methods • Systematicity of observations and data collections • Interrater reliability of transcript content and coding • Estimations of data collection obtrusiveness • Thick descriptions • Analysis of researcher's role • Expert debriefing
Confirmability *Basis of findings can be traced through the data set*	• Theory grounded in data • Logical inferences • Clear reasonings for category identification • Accommodate negative evidence	• Audit trail • Triangulation • Peer debriefing • Expert debriefing • Systematicity of observations and data collections • Member check • Interrater reliability

Source: Reprinted by permission, Baker (1995).

researcher's perspective, who collected and analyzed data in only one classroom for a specified duration of time, informed by one theoretical lens. In addition, the study examined the nature of literacy in a technology-rich setting—yet technology is ever changing. Thus, readers must consider the evolution of technology as used in this study when considering transfer to other settings that have newer technologies. Finally, this was my first foray into formulating and conducting my own research. So, researcher sophistication, while stated as a concern with purposeful methods used to address the concern, remained a reality. The goal of a design is to be as strategic as possible and then enunciate the limitations of the design. While you should embrace every possible strategy to make your work trustworthy, you must remain aware of ways your work may not be trustworthy and remind your readers of these limitations.

If you are tempted to skip or skimp on the necessary work to identify the concerns and methods to address trustworthiness of your study, I encourage you to not bother with conducting your study. Why expend the time and resources necessary for conducting your work only to have all outlets reject your findings because they are not trustworthy? Instead, double down on efforts to identify all possible threats to the trustworthiness of your work. Ask as many experts as you can to expose threats to the trustworthiness of your work. Then, formulate strategies to undergird the trustworthiness of your work. Be strategic. Not only do you want outlets such as journals and funding agencies to esteem your findings, but you also want to value your findings.

Logistics: Gatekeepers, Timelines, Phases, and Budget

Table 5.2 includes a final methodology section dedicated to logistics. These are the plans you need to make to launch your study. Begin with the gatekeepers. If you are affiliated with a university, this will include your Institutional Review Board (IRB). Secure your IRB forms and schedule before you complete your proposal. This will allow you to add topics to your proposal that you may have omitted (e.g., participant consent letters). It is best to know what is required by your IRB sooner rather than later. In addition, some IRBs meet occasionally. You will want to be on their calendar instead of waiting to initiate your study because you are not on their calendar.

I find it helpful to create timelines. When do you plan to initiate conversations with the setting gatekeepers? When do you anticipate clearance from all gatekeepers (e.g., IRB and setting) so that you can make initial contact with potential participants? How long do you anticipate it will take to identify germane participants and secure their consent? I recommend that you think of your study in terms of phases. Every tradition will have its own set of phases. Table 5.6 aligns phases with the sample question which used ethnographic research methods. I find that phases overlap and are often concurrent as well as recursive. Nonetheless, if you formulate phases of inquiry with a projected timeline, it may help you identify where you are in the process.

Finally, all studies require time and resources. Before you launch your study, do yourself a favor by considering what you will need to complete your study.

TABLE 5.6 ■ Common Phases: Ethnographic Studies

Phases	Foci of Phase
Phase 1: Become familiar with setting	• Initiate data collection and analysis methods • Identify rhythm of activities (e.g., class schedule) • Become familiar with the structure of activities (e.g., instructional methods) • Become familiar with participant interactions • Negotiate role with participants • Consider obtrusiveness • Define data collection unit (define the parameters of data)
Phase 2: Focused exploration to formulate provisional hypotheses	• Refine data collection and analysis methods • Refine data collection unit • Refine data collection methods • Identify provisional patterns • Formulate provisional hypotheses
Phase 3: Refined exploration to formalize hypotheses	• Develop, refine, confirm, and disconfirm hypotheses • Conduct theoretical sampling • Conduct member checks • Debrief with peers and/or experts • Conduct negative case analysis
Phase 4: Confirmed exploration to establish redundancy	• Continue to refine, confirm, and disconfirm hypotheses • Triangulate across artifacts, interviews, and observations • Triangulate across participants • Continue to conduct negative case analysis • Develop report

Maybe one of the first items on your timeline is to secure funding. You might need funding for your time. Estimate how much time each day you will need. Determine how you can protect and dedicate that time. What time do you need to complete this study? Data collection in the field is only a portion of the time needed to process the data. If you collect observation notes, you will need time to expand those notes into complete thoughts and narratives. If you conduct interviews, you will need time to transcribe them. If you collect video, you will need time to document their contents. If you collect artifacts, you will need a cataloging process. Personally, I prefer to catalog, index, and cross-reference all data sets. I want to be able to code observation notes and immediately access corresponding artifacts and transcripts. It is easy to lose precious time simply finding data. Give yourself the time and organizational tools to keep up with your data. Your tradition will help you ascertain the resources you will need.

WELCOME TO A NEW FRONTIER: SUMMARY AND CONCLUSION

Congratulations! You are now ready to finalize your proposal and pursue a new frontier: your study! Using the Anatomy of a Qualitative Research Question, you identified the elements of your study: paradigm, interrogative, topic, setting, perspective, and research tradition with corresponding genre for your research report. You did some metaphysical introspection to determine your view of reality. You considered whether to pose a *Who, What, Where, When, Why,* or *How* question. You substituted sundry settings for your study to identify who your participants might be. You took the time to make your tacit assumptions about your topic explicit and situated yourself among theoretical perspectives either within and/or beyond your field. You considered the implications of conducting your study as a case study versus an ethnography versus a phenomenology versus multiple research traditions commonly used in your field. You systematically made substitutions to each part of the Anatomy and rephrased your research question accordingly. You stepped back and took a look at your emerging research question and aligned the parts of the Anatomy to make sure there was a fit between them. You continued to tweak your research question by generating potential answers to your question as well as the genre of your final report.

Given a solid grasp of what your research question might be, you considered ways to be intentionally innovative by creating new intersections of previously unrelated parts of the Anatomy. You used the Anatomy to structure the significance of your study as a tightly orchestrated rationale. You used the Anatomy to identify the constructs of your conceptual framework and thereby avoided meandering into the forest of tangentially fascinating topics with a potential list of other studies to conduct. Finally, you formulated your methodology. You are poised to flesh out your proposal! You have completed the groundwork. You have laid a foundation. You have embraced the prequel to qualitative research.

At the beginning of this book, I argued that your research question is the essence, the progenitor of your study. I argued that your research question, if well formulated, contained all of the necessary design elements of your study. Once you have a solid question, the design of your study is self-evident. I am hopeful that you can now see my point. Of course, as you begin to collect and analyze data, you may continue to revise your research question. That's OK! Hopefully, your continued revisions will be strategic as you consider ways to ask and pursue significant research.

At the beginning of this book, I argued that an understanding of the Anatomy would not only help you formulate a qualitative research question but also facilitate conversations with coresearchers. Given a common understanding of the Anatomy, a research team can have conversations about paradigms, interrogatives, topics, settings, perspectives, and research traditions with corresponding research report genres. When the team purposely engages in conversations about how to substitute the parts of the Anatomy, I am hopeful everyone will understand how to strategically hone the research question and thereby push forward the design and common understanding of the purpose of the study. In fact, conversations may reveal how the team parses and takes lead of various Anatomy parts or substitutions. For example, maybe members purposely collect, analyze, and interpret data from different theoretical perspectives thus enriching the implications of the study.

Finally, I argued that the Anatomy could help qualitative researchers hone their ability to review manuscripts. Whether you are a reviewer for a peer-reviewed journal, conference, or funding agency, the Anatomy may help you identify the strengths of a proposal or manuscript as well as provide succinct yet helpful suggestions for the author(s). If you are in a position to mentor qualitative researchers, I hope that the Anatomy will also give you and your mentees a common language and process for crafting the essence of a qualitative study. It is my intention that the Anatomy helps seasoned and novice researchers craft studies that unveil their passions with the potential to push your understanding of reality forward. Such is the purpose and essence of research.

SUGGESTED ACTIVITIES AND DISCUSSIONS

1. Identify 10+ studies that are related to your question. As you move toward a full proposal this list will grow. Fill out Worksheet 5.1. Then evaluate the commonalities

across studies related to the Anatomy. Do most of the studies employ similar paradigms, interrogatives, settings, perspective(s), and research traditions? Use your evaluation to either revise your question or assert how your work builds on and extends the existing literature. Use your evaluation to articulate how your work advances a nascent intersection of previously unrelated constructs (e.g., ice skates + roller skates = roller blades). When your study is complete, use Worksheet 5.1 to help you elaborate the Discussion section of your reports.

2. Before you write your proposal, fill out Worksheets 5.2 and 5.3. Use Worksheet 5.2 to engage in productive conversations with mentors, colleagues, friends, and family members. Some may not be willing or able to read and provide feedback on full proposals. Using Worksheet 5.2 you may be able to elicit invaluable feedback.
3. As you craft your proposal, be sure to plan for methodological trustworthiness. Based on the research tradition, or an amalgamation of methods, you plan to use, identify the methodological concerns for trustworthiness and strategically plan to address each concern (e.g., Table 5.5). Complete Worksheet 5.3. As you strategize, you may need to revise Worksheet 5.2.
4. Refine your rationale by giving your elevator speech to as many unsuspecting bystanders as you can. If you are in a doctoral seminar reading and discussing this book, then pair off and give your sales pitch to a different classmate every 2 minutes. Do this a few times and then debrief with those who heard your pitch. As you refine your research question and proposal, you might do this brief activity for several weeks. If you are a researcher reading this book, find colleagues and family for the same exercise. Be sure to ask them how you can hone your pitch.
5. Watch the online documentary *Margaret Mead and Samoa* (at the time of this printing, https://www.youtube.com/watch?v=GOCYhmnx6o8). Using Worksheet 5.3, examine and discuss the video as it relates to each concern and criterion for trustworthiness.
6. Plan for trustworthiness. Using a research question that you generated for Worksheet 3.1, complete Worksheet 5.3. Based on your research tradition (e.g., ethnography), what are the concerns for each criterion? What data collection and research methods do you plan to invoke to address these concerns? What concerns remain? If you are unaware of the concerns and criterion for trustworthiness, then mark the information you need to complete Worksheet 5.3. Use these marks to collect this information as you design your study. It is never too late to start to collect the concerns and strategies to undergird trustworthiness for your data collection and analysis methods.

SUGGESTED RESOURCES

Heimans, F. (1988). *Margaret Mead and Samoa [Video]*. YouTube. Retrieved from https://youtu.be/GOCYhmnx6o8.

Lincoln, Y. S., & Guba, E. G. (1985). Establishing trustworthiness. In *Naturalistic inquiry* (pp. 289–331). Thousand Oaks, CA: SAGE.

WORKSHEET 5.1 ■ Examine Innovation and Significance

Identify studies related to your question. Fill out Worksheet 5.1 to consider how your question compares. Add as many rows as you need. Use this comparison to formulate your rationale. After you conduct your study, use this comparison to discuss your findings and significance.

Author(s) and Publication Year	Question/Purpose Rationale	CF (Perspective + Constructs)	Paradigm Epistemology Ontology	Tradition and Report Genre	Data Sources, Collection, and Role	Data Analysis	Trustworthiness

WORKSHEET 5.2 ■ Proposal Worksheet

Fill out the following information. Limit: 1 page. No narrative. Simply list.

Rationale: Question/Purpose Statement

Given A:
Given B:
Given ...
Therefore, <insert question/purpose>

Optional, Delimitations

Conceptual Framework
List theoretical perspective(s) and substantive constructs

Paradigm

Research Tradition

Setting and Participants

Data you plan to collect

Types of data analysis you plan to use

Trustworthiness
Include Worksheet 5.3, Trustworthiness (e.g., Table 5.5, Ethnographic Trustworthiness: Corresponding Criteria, Concerns, and Methods)

Gatekeepers
List who you need to negotiate with to begin data collection

Phases and timeline
List the phases and projected timeline for each phase (may include another sheet)

Anticipated findings
Brainstorm and list 3–5 findings that may emerge from your study

Genre
What literary style will you use to write up your study?

WORKSHEET 5.3 ■ Trustworthiness

What are the concerns inherent in your design/tradition? What methods will you use to address each concern?

Criteria	Concerns	Methods
Credibility *Truth value, capable of being believed*		
Transferability *Ability to infer implications from research to other settings*		
Dependability *Used methods as specified*		
Confirmability *Basis of findings can be traced through the data set*		

REFERENCES

Baker, E. A. (1995). The nature of literacy activities in a high technology environment from a meaning making perspective. (Doctoral dissertation. Peabody College of Vanderbilt University.) *UMI Dissertation Services*, 9539919.

Baker, E. A. (2001). The nature of literacy in a technology-rich, fourth-grade classroom. *Reading Research and Instruction*, 40(3), 159–184.

Baker, E. A. (2007). Elementary classroom web sites: Support for literacy within and beyond the classroom. *Journal of Literacy Research*, 39(1), 1–38.

Baker, E. A. (Ed.) (2010). *The new literacies: Multiple perspectives on research and practice*. New York, NY: Guilford.

Baker, E. A. (2017). Apps, iPads, and literacy: Examining the feasibility of speech recognition in a first-grade classroom. *Reading Research Quarterly*, 52(3). doi: 10.1002/rrq.170

Baker, E. A. (2020, December). Wag the Dog: A digital literacies narrative. Presidential address presented at the meeting of the Literacy Research Association. Retrieved from https://youtu.be/Avzup21ZnA4

Baker, E. A., Alfayez, A., Dalton, C., McInnish, R. S., Schwerdtfeger, R., & Khajeloo, M. (2015). The irrevocable alteration of communication: A glimpse into the societal impact of digital media. In B. Guzzetti, & M. Lesley (Eds.), *Handbook of research on the societal impact of digital media* (pp. 94–126). Hershey, PA: IGI Global.

Baker, E. A., Rozendal, M., & Whitenack, J. (2000). Audience awareness in a technology rich elementary classroom. *Journal of Literacy Research*, 32(3), 395–419.

Birks, M., & Mills, J. (2015). *Grounded theory: A practical guide* (2nd ed.). London: SAGE.

Bransford, J. D., & Johnson, M. K. (1972). Contextual prerequisites for understanding: Some investigations of comprehension and recall. *Journal of Verbal Learning and Verbal Behavior*, 11(6), 717–726.

Charmaz, K. (2006). *Constructing grounded theory: A practical guide through qualitative analysis*. Thousand Oaks, CA: SAGE.

Chilisa, B. (2011). *Indigenous research methodologies*. Thousand Oaks, CA: SAGE.

Clandinin, D. J. (Ed.) (2007). *Handbook of narrative inquiry: Mapping a methodology*. Thousand Oaks, CA: SAGE. doi:10.4135/9781452226552

Clandinin, D. J., & Huber, J. (2010). Narrative inquiry. In B. McGaw, E. Baker, & P. P. Peterson (Eds.), *International encyclopaedia of education* (3rd ed.). New York, NY: Elsevier.

Creswell, J. W. (2017). *Qualitative inquiry and research design: Choosing among five traditions* (4th ed.). Thousand Oaks, CA: SAGE.

Denzin, N. K., & Lincoln, Y. S. (2005). Introduction: The discipline and practice of qualitative research. In N. K. Denzin, & Y. S. Lincoln (Eds.), *Handbook of qualitative research* (3rd ed., pp. 1–32). Thousand Oaks, CA: SAGE.

Denzin, N. K., & Lincoln, Y. S. (2018). Introduction: The discipline and practice of qualitative research. In N. K. Denzin, & Y. S. Lincoln (Eds.), *Handbook of qualitative research* (5th ed., pp. 1–26). Thousand Oaks, CA: SAGE.

Descartes, R. (1637). *Discourse on the method of rightly conducting one's reason and of seeking truth in the sciences*. Retrieved from http://www.gutenberg.org/files/59/59-h/59-h.htm

Einstein, A. (1982, August). How I created the theory of relativity (PDF). *Physics Today*, 45–47. Retrieved from https://pdfs.semanticscholar.org/4ed5/c3077e53023171928b537ed71d017f295a5a.pdf

Geertz, C. (1993). *Local knowledge: Further essays in interpretive anthropology*. London: Fontana.

Glaser, B. G. (1965). The constant comparative method of qualitative analysis. *Social Problems*, 12(4), 436–445.

Guba, E. G., & Lincoln, Y. S. (1994). Competing paradigms in qualitative research. In N. K. Denzin, & Y. S. Lincoln (Eds.), *Handbook of qualitative research* (pp. 105–117). Thousand Oaks, CA: SAGE.

Hatch, J. A. (2002). *Doing qualitative research in education settings*. Albany, NY: State University of New York Press.

Heimans, F. (1988). *Margaret mead and Samoa [Video]*. YouTube. Retrieved from https://youtu.be/GOCYhmnx6o8

Kivunja, C., & Kuyini, A. B. (2017). Understanding and applying research paradigms in educational contexts. *International Journal of Higher Education*, 6(5), 26–41.

Lincoln, Y. S., & Guba, E. G. (1985a). *Naturalistic inquiry*. Thousand Oaks, CA: SAGE.

Lincoln, Y. S., & Guba, E. G. (1985b). Establishing trustworthiness. In *Naturalistic inquiry* (pp. 289–331). Thousand Oaks, CA: SAGE.

Lincoln, Y. S., & Guba, E. G. (2005). Paradigmatic controversies, contradictions, and emerging confluences. In N. K. Denzin, & Y. S. Lincoln (Eds.), *The SAGE handbook of qualitative research* (pp. 191–215). Thousand Oaks, CA: SAGE.

Morgan, D. L. (2014). Pragmatism as a paradigm for social research. *Qualitative Inquiry*, 20(8), 1045–1053. doi:10.1177/1077800413513733

Moustakas, C. E. (1961). *Loneliness*. Englewood Cliffs, NJ: Prentice-Hall.

Moustakas, C. E. (1994). *Phenomenological research methods*. Thousand Oaks, CA: SAGE.

Patton, M. Q. (2014). *Qualitative research and evaluation methods* (4th ed.). Thousand Oaks, CA: SAGE.

Quint, J. (1963). The impact of mastectomy. *American Journal of Nursing*, 63(11), 88–92.

Rumelhart, D. E. (1980). Schemata: The building blocks of cognition. In R. J. Spiro, B. C. Bruce, W. F. Brewer (Eds.), *Theoretical issues in reading comprehension* (pp. 33–58). Hillsdale, NJ: Erlbaum. 9781315107493. doi:10.4324/9781315107493-4

Seidman, I. (2019). *Interviewing as qualitative research: A guide for researchers in education and social sciences* (5th ed.). New York, NY: Teachers College Press.

Steffe, L. P., & Gale, J. E. (Eds.) (1995). *Constructivism in education*. Hillsdale, NJ: Lawrence Erlbaum Associates.

Strauss, A., & Corbin, J. (1990). *Basics of qualitative research: Grounded theory procedures and techniques*. Thousand Oaks, CA: SAGE.

van Manen, M. (2014). *Phenomenology of practice*. Walnut Creek, CA: Left Coast Press.

Wolcott, H. F. (2009). *Writing up qualitative research* (3rd ed.). Thousand Oaks, CA: SAGE. doi:10.4135/9781452234878

Appendix A

KEY TERMS

A priori Coding. A data analysis strategy whereby the researcher codes data according to preexisting codes.

Biography. A research tradition designed to study a particular person's life story from birth to present/death.

Case Study. A research tradition designed to study person(s) or event(s) bounded by time within specified contexts which may invoke quantitative and qualitative data collection and analyses and can have a large scope (e.g., within a country, across a decade) or small scope (e.g., among a group of children in a specific classroom during a specific activity).

Conceptual Framework. A section of research proposals and reports that delineates the precipice of theoretical perspectives and substantive constructs related to the study.

Confirmability. A criterion of trustworthiness that allows researchers and readers to trace the derivation of findings through the data set. Answers the question: Are the findings derived from the data?

Constructivism. A research paradigm that believes reality is ascribed by the human experience to the knower.

Content Analysis. A research tradition that relies predominantly on collecting and analyzing artifact data. Some use the same term to describe a data analysis method of artifact data.

Credibility. A criterion of trustworthiness that requires researchers to employ strategies that establish the truth value of the findings and justification that the findings are capable of being believed. Answers the question: Were data collection and analysis robust enough to tease out misinformation, researcher's cultural and methodological naissance, ascertain atypical events, and build trust?

Critical. A research paradigm that views reality as power and existence as political whereby research is an emancipatory act that demands change.

DCU (Data Collection Unit). The criterion used to ascertain what constitutes data for your study. Answers the questions: Where do data begin and end? What is coded and what is not coded? Why?

Delimitations. An explanation of what the study is not about.

Dependability. A criterion of trustworthiness that requires researchers to employ strategies that establish whether the research methods were used as specified and conform to established procedures. Answers the question: Was the research plan followed?

Epistemology. The philosophy of the existence of knowledge.

Ethnography. A research tradition designed to study culture.

Genre (Report Genre). Literary style that aligns with research methods. For example, if you conduct a biographical study, you will write a biographical report.

Grounded Theory. A research tradition that seeks to theorize the origins of a topic to predict the future of that topic (e.g., Darwin's theory of the origins of species). However, others use the same term for findings that are derived from (grounded in) the data.

Heuristic. A technique, strategy for accomplishing a task.

Limitations. The inadequacies inherent to the research design (e.g., from specified perspective(s), in particular setting, during specific timeframe) in which findings should be contextualized.

Methodology. The philosophy and corresponding methods used to conduct a study which includes a description of how paradigmatic assumptions and research methods align.

Methods (Research Method). The steps to follow as you collect and analyze data. Some use **tradition** and **method** interchangeably while others distinguish between these terms (see Tradition).

Narrative Inquiry. A research tradition designed to study participants' stories (e.g., journals, autobiographies, memoirs, conversations, photographs) which may include the researcher as part of the stories.

Ontology. The philosophy of existence or being. Descartes' (1637) argument for reality, *I think therefore I am*, is an example of an ontological statement.

Open Coding. A data analysis strategy whereby the researcher specifies their theoretical perspective(s) and codes accordingly with the goal of generating characteristics, categories, and themes across the data set.

Paradigm. The coalescence of ontology, epistemology, research tradition, and report genre which formulate your understanding of truth and reality. Deeply held convictions that explain reality. Your worldview. The categorization of paradigms differs across theorists and remains organic and fluid. For the purposes of this book, paradigms are categorized and described as positivism, postpositivism, constructivism, critical, and poststructural.

Perspective (Theoretical Perspective, Lens). Point of view that defines how you see your topic, informs when data occur (e.g., if topic is literacy—my perspective informs what I code as "literacy" and what I do not code), and may provide tenets for your rationale as well as significance of your findings. (See Chapter 1, *Perspective: Sociocultural*)

Phenomenology. A research tradition designed to examine a lived experience of a phenomena (e.g., loneliness, turning points, graduate school).

Positivism. A research paradigm that believes reality exists regardless of human experience; thus systematic data collection and analysis can reveal reality and findings can be generalized.

Postpositivism. A research paradigm that believes reality is expansive, thus systematic data collection and analysis provide an estimation of reality.

Poststructuralism. A research paradigm that questions systematized research methods that produce tenets—especially if the tenets define reality, reify current conceptions, or produce binaries.

Prolonged Engagement. A description of the role of the researcher whereby the researcher becomes part of the culture by being consistently present and involved in substantive activities with the participants. This role is distinct from longitudinal methods in which researchers drop by over extended periods of time (e.g., collect pre–post measures).

Thick Description. Refers to a research report that includes sufficient description of the setting and social norms such that readers can compare the study to their own settings.

Tradition (Research Tradition). Cohesive orchestration of a set of data collection and data analysis methods that coalesce to address specific types of questions while mitigating threats to trustworthiness.

Transferability. A criterion of trustworthiness that requires researchers to employ strategies that allow readers to relate research findings to other settings. Answers the question: Can the findings provide insights for other settings?

Trustworthiness. Reasons the findings of a qualitative study are believable. While quantitative studies seek to be valid and reliable, qualitative studies seek to be credible, transferable, dependable, and confirmable.

Appendix B

RESEARCH PARADIGMS: ONTOLOGY, EPISTEMOLOGY, METHODOLOGY, TRADITIONS, AND PRODUCTS

Paradigms (Worldviews)	**Ontology** (Nature of reality)	**Epistemology** (What can be known; Relationship of knower and known)	**Methodology** (How knowledge is gained)	**Research Traditions** (Coherent data collection and analysis strategies that address inherent design threats)	**Products** (Forms of knowledge produced)
Positivist	Reality exists regardless of human experience	**How the world is really ordered; Knower is distinct from known;** Findings are generalizable	**Experimental** **Quasi-experimental**	Surveys Correlational studies Statistical modeling Growth Curve Analysis	**Facts, theories, laws, predictions**, cause-effect
Pragmatist	*Nonsingular*	*Relational*	*Mixed Methods*	Varied combinations of Positivistic and Nonpositivistic traditions	Varied combinations of Positivistic and Nonpositivistic traditions
Postpositivist	Reality is expansive; systematic analyses facilitate the ability to make estimations of reality	**Approximations of reality;** the researcher and researched cannot be isolated therefore researcher bias must be acknowledged; findings are contextual and therefore not generalizable but may be transferable	**Rigorously defined qualitative methods that may include frequency counts and low-level statistics** Naturalistic Situated experiments	Action Research Biography Case Study Content Analysis Autoethnography Duoethnography Ethnography Formative/Teaching/Design Experiments Grounded Theory Narrative Inquiry Phenomenology Self-study **NOTE*	Research Traditions invoke corresponding genres which typically include varied combinations of descriptions, patterns, coalesced themes, narratives, interpretations, and reconstructions (e.g., biographical studies produce biographies)
Constructivist	Reality is ascribed by the human experience	**Knowledge is a human construction; Researcher and participant coconstruct understandings**			
Critical	Reality is power; existence is political	Research is an emancipatory act that demands change; **Researchers' values frame the inquiry**	**Transformative inquiry** *Dialogic*		**Value mediated critiques that challenge existing power structures and promote resistance**
Poststructuralist	**There is no "Truth" to be known;** Reality is plural and fluid; reality may be chaotic and illogical; concepts of reality must be interrogated for reification and binaries	**Researchers examine the world through textual representations of it;** At its core, knowledge is limited and instable	**Deconstruction** **Data-based multivoiced studies**	Metatheory	**Deconstructions** **Reflexive, polyvocal texts**

Hatch (2002)
Kivunja & Kuyini (2017)
Baker (this volume)
**NOTE: Research traditions may align with a range of paradigms (see Chapter 1)*

INDEX

Milton Keynes UK
Ingram Content Group UK Ltd.
UKHW022012100823
426697UK00013B/244